1

On the Primitive Way

Two Texan Brothers Journey to Santiago

Landon Roussel

Communitas Press

On the Primitive Way
Written by Landon Roussel.
Edited by Harte Weiner.
© Cover design by Christina Rodriguez.

Published by **Communitas Press 2015**

Lutcher, Louisiana

This work is a non-fiction memoir. As much as possible has been done to describe facts, events and details with historical accuracy.

ISBN-10: 0-9969681-0-5
ISBN-13: 978-0-9969681-0-2
Library of Congress Control Number 2015919521

For Cory, who encouraged me to never stop trying reconnect with those we love most.

Praise for *On the Primitive Way*

"*On the Primitive Way* is the first Camino memoir to chronicle not only the Way of Saint James but also the way of two brothers: their separation, reuniting and healing on their pilgrimage."
—Martin Sheen, award-winning actor starring in *The Way* (2010)

"After eleven centuries of history, the pilgrimage still has the ability to work 'miracles.' This is what Cory and Landon experienced as pilgrims in *On the Primitive Way*. Passing the seven mountain passes that occur between Oviedo and Santiago, a metaphor for the difficulties in life they had to overcome, they were able to find at the end: peace, true brotherhood and harmony with nature."
—Antón Pombo Rodriguez, best-selling author of *Camino* guidebooks

"If you've walked El Camino from Saint Jean, *On the Primitive Way* will make you want to walk it from Oviedo."
—Kurt Koontz, author of *A Million Steps*

"*On the Primitive Way* is more than another Camino memoir, it is a story of two brothers, estranged by addiction and reconciled on the Way. Anyone who has had a family member or loved on suffering from addiction will relate to Landon's description of his struggle to love his brother even when he continues to fall deeper into substance abuse."
—Beatriz Gonzales-Stephan, Lee Hage Jamail Chair in Latin American Studies, Rice University

Map of the Primitive Way of Saint James

Stages (*Etapas*) of the Primitive Way

1: Oviedo—San Juan de Villapañada
(30.5 kilometers, 18.8 miles)

2: San Juan de Villapañada—Salas
(20.2 kilometers, 12.4 miles)

3: Salas—Tineo
(20.2 kilometers, 12.4 miles)

4: Tineo—Pola de Allande
(28.2 kilometers, 17.4 miles)

5: Pola de Allande—La Mesa (just past Berducedo)
(22.8 kilometers, 14.0 miles)

6: La Mesa—Grandas de Salime
(16.8 kilometers, 10.8 miles)

7: Grandas de Salime—Padrón (Fonsagrada)
(28.1 kilometers, 17.3 miles)

8: Padrón (Fonsagrada)—O Cadavo (Baleira)
(23.4 kilometers, 14.4 miles)

9: O Cadavo (Baleira)—Lugo
(30.5 kilometers, 18.8 miles)

10: Lugo—San Roman de Retorta
(19.7 kilometers, 12.1 miles)

11:San Roman de Retorta—Melide
(27.7 kilometers, 16.7 miles)

12: Melide— O Pedrouzo (just after Santa Irene)
(33.3 kilometers, 20.5 miles)

13: O Pedrouzo—Santiago
(20 kilometers, 12.3 miles)

Table of Contents

Commonly used Spanish words

Albergue: a hostel

Flecha: an arrow

Concha: a seashell

Mochila: a backpack

Hospitalero: a caretaker

Camino: a way or path

Etapa: a stage or step

Credencial: a pilgrim passport

1.

Chains Stronger Than Steel

"We forge the chains we wear in life."
—Charles Dickens

Baton Rouge, Louisiana
Tuesday, February 5, 2013

I was sitting on the living room couch when my mom, standing in the kitchen nearby, received an unexpected phone call. I could hear her from the living room, where I sat holding my infant son in one hand and sipping espresso with the other.

"What?" she yelled emphatically. "Tomorrow?" she went on.

From the tone of her voice, I could tell she was talking to my younger brother, Cory. She paced back and forth a couple of times in the kitchen before retreating to her bedroom.

I sat on the sofa still holding baby Benny in my arms. He was awake, wide-eyed and almost smiling. The morning had been relaxing so far. My wife Amanda and I were visiting my parents in Baton Rouge during my wife's maternity leave. We had no particular plans for the day other than to enjoy our time together.

About ten minutes later, Mom came back from the living room to tell me the news – Cory was going to be released from prison the following day. His release had been scheduled for two weeks later, but for reasons unbeknownst to us, the Bureau of Prisons was going to release him the following morning. He would be released from the Metropolitan Correctional Center (MCC) in San Diego and sent on a bus to San Antonio, where he was expected to present himself two days later at a halfway house.

"That's great, but what are we going to do about our flights for next weekend?" I responded.

My mother, father and I had already made travel arrangements to visit Cory two weeks later on his scheduled release date. We would have to cancel these. More than that, should he be immediately sent to a halfway house, neither I nor Amanda nor my son Benny—who Cory had not yet met—would have the chance to see him for quite some time. My mom had informed me that he would not have visitation privileges when he got to the halfway house. Thus, we wouldn't be able to see him until he was released well over a month later. This meant that I would not be able to see him for almost two month since I was scheduled to leave for London in three weeks for a month-long medical school rotation at a general practice clinic.

"Can he take a flight here?" I asked my mom. This would give him a couple of days to spend with us in Baton Rouge before going to San Antonio. Our parents or I could then drive him to San Antonio when he had to be there.

"Well, that's what I'm looking into. He could. The only problem is that all his belongings are here. He doesn't even have a photo ID to board a plane."

"Is there any way we could overnight mail it to someone we know and have them bring it to him?" I asked.

"Well, we don't know anyone in San Diego well enough to do that, but maybe we can mail it to a shipping center that receives mail. I'll look into that. Could you look into one-way flights from San Diego for me?"

She left the room. Holding Benny in my arms, I beckoned Amanda to come to the living room. I told her about Cory's impending release and our dilemma with not being able to see him. "Do what you need to help your brother," she said.

I handed Benny over to her and grabbed my mom's laptop from the coffee table. I began to search for flights. Before I could even think about a concrete flight itinerary to book him, I began to have second thoughts about the plan. I was not confident that Cory would actually get his ID. Sending a letter quick enough to arrive the next morning would be difficult to arrange without a clear recipient. Plus, Cory had no phone or internet access to contact us if he had trouble locating the pick-up spot.

Were he unable to get through airport security—God forbid he was on an FBI 'No fly' list—he would have no way to make it to the bus on time. He could potentially be arrested again for failing to show up at the halfway house. Moreover, Cory was not known for making travel plans run smoothly. No, this idea was not going to work out.

There had to be a simpler way to get him to fly back. As his older brother, I wanted to make it happen. We hadn't seen each other for nearly two years, and he had just been through the roughest two years of his life in prison. The least I could do for him was to make sure that he had a couple of days with his new nephew. It was not that I felt I owed it to him, but being my brother, it felt only natural to extend to him the kindness of helping him transition back into society. If he couldn't count on me, whom could he count on?

The only choice that seemed safe enough to ensure that he got to the halfway house on time and still got to see us was for me to fly to San Diego myself. To try to arrange for him to get his ID from a postal center and fly back on his own left too much to chance. While I could ask my mom to fly to San Diego later in the day, she had flown there several times after his arrest, conviction and imprisonment. I, unfortunately, had not been able to visit him, as I was in medical school and then a graduate student in Europe while he was in prison. Moreover, frequent traveling was not unusual for me that year. I was already commuting at least once a month from Houston, where my wife was teaching high school, to New York where I was enrolled in my last year of medical school.

I beckoned Amanda again from our bedroom to tell her my idea. Even though I was on vacation from medical school, this was no small endeavor for our family. Our son Benny was less than two months old, and I had never spent a night away from him before. He was not sleeping through the night. She needed my help to change diapers and heat up milk. Nonetheless, when I explained to her my idea to bring the ID to him myself, she was quite sympathetic.

"I want Benny to meet his uncle," she said. "If this is what it takes for him to see Uncle Cory this week, you should go. It is the right thing to do."

Having settled on me going to San Diego, I called my mom to the living room to explain my proposal. She was more than happy with it. Within minutes I booked the next available flight for San Diego. Round trips were only available from Houston later in the afternoon. Amanda quickly packed my bags. Within an hour from Cory's phone call, I was driving to Houston's Intercontinental Airport with Cory's ID in my bag. Driving to the airport, I was confident I had not forgotten a thing, until three hours into the trip—in Beaumont—I recalled that I left my espresso half-finished on the coffee table.

***

Beaumont, TX

March 2004

I could feel my heart pounding in my chest wall as I pulled my car into the parking lot at West Brook High School in Beaumont. I had just drank a strong cup of coffee that morning. Coffee drinking was not a usual habit of mine, but I had been using it the past few weeks to stay up to study. That day I had an economics test, the results of which would have a major impact on my grade. I was up until three o'clock in the morning studying.

I had never experienced this type of reaction to coffee. Was I having a heart attack? Was it an irregular rhythm? I didn't know. Fear gripped me as I imagined the worst-case scenarios.

This was it. I wasn't going to drink coffee anymore. Eighteen was too young to be drinking coffee. Pretty soon I would be addicted. True, coffee is an innocuous addiction, but at the time the danger of any drug addiction—even caffeine—aroused all too fresh fears for me. Addiction had led astray the other usual passenger in the car—the person who was supposed to be sitting next to me, Cory. I did not want to go down the same path as my little brother, who was spending the last three months of his junior year of high school at an intensive drug rehab facility in North Texas.

Cory had begun smoking marijuana at the age of eleven. This led to drinking and other drugs. None of us in the family found out about his drug use, however, until he was sixteen.

Mutual friends would tell me that he and I were 'different' from each other. I was incredibly focused, spending most of my free time studying to get the best grades as possible and making the decision as a freshman that I wanted to become a doctor. Cory, while incredibly smart, was not focused. He eked by with "C"s in his classes and had no idea whether he even wanted to go to college.

When rumors circulated that he might be using drugs, I had trouble believing them. I just thought he was running with different crowds. During my senior year, however, a mutual acquaintance told me that Cory had gotten drunk on rum in a Dr. Pepper can at the last football game. Not wanting to be a snitch, however, I refrained from passing along any hearsay to my parents. I didn't want to get him in trouble for what seemed like just typical high school mischief. I reasoned at the time that was okay with me if he was different, as long as he was not hurting anyone.

However, it became evident that this was more than just "normal" high school drinking. His substance use clearly started impacting our family's relationship with him. By the time Cory was a high school junior, he was having daily outbursts of anger, slept through the family Christmas gathering and perpetually isolated himself in his room. Still I resisted getting involved. I loved him deeply, and did not want to give him any reason to think that I rejected him for being different.

One day in January of my senior year, I overheard Cory through the bathroom door describe to his friend 'a sweet joint'. By then, enough was enough. He was spending most of his time as a sixteen year-old high school junior getting high. He was clearly heading for rock bottom. After overhearing him, I wrote a letter to my mom explaining to her my suspicion of his drug use.

When my parents confronted him, he insisted that it was his right to do drugs.

My parents tried grounding him, taking away all privileges and even putting him under house arrest. Mom even confiscated his cell phone and called the parents of his contacts, informing them that Cory was using drugs and that their children might be dabbling too. Still, nothing seemed to dampen his drive for drugs.

One Saturday night, my parents went on a church retreat, leaving me with strict instructions to tell them if he left home for any other reason than to go to work. When I dropped him off in the parking lot at his work, he told me that he was not coming home and that if I even dared to tell our mom and dad, he threatened, "I will fucking kill you."

That night, I broke out in tears while driving to a friend's house—whose mother was gracious enough to let me sleep in a guestroom. I pulled over on the side of the highway, desperately hoping a police officer would flag me down. I wanted to tell someone, anyone, how much it hurt to be threatened by a brother I deeply loved. Eventually, when no police officer pulled behind me, I called our mom. "I can't do it any more," I sobbed. "I can't live like this…in constant fear of my own brother."

"It's okay," she said. "We're going to work it out."

But, it didn't work out. Cory kept coming home whenever he pleased—sometimes high, sometimes angry. I could barely talk to him without stirring up an angry backlash. Anytime I heard our parents talking to my brother downstairs, I feared that his wrath would get out of hand. Once when I was doing homework in our study, I overheard them arguing in the living room. He wanted to go out and do drugs. They wouldn't let him. He stormed out anyway. I remember Mom saying to Dad after Cory stomped out, slamming the front door behind him, that "we can't let this keep going on. We have to do something."

Later that week a big, bulky man from church—also a father of a teenager with substance abuse problems—and our pastor came to our house, and along with our dad, forced Cory into the pastor's Suburban to take him to the nearest psychiatric hospital with a substance abuse treatment wing. In the process, Dad got a black eye. Cory was involuntarily committed. As a minor, my parents were able to do this. He was not, however, suicidal, psychotic, manic or floridly depressed. They just didn't know what to do and needed help.

For the first week, Cory refused to back down on his "right" to do drugs. After a week, he learned to play the game. He agreed to quit using drugs for the immediate future. He still saw no problem with drug use but agreed to cease until he was out of my parents' house. He was sent home on a mood-stabilizing medication and told to follow up with a psychiatrist.

However, when he got home, he refused to take medication or see a shrink. Cory was using drugs within weeks at most, and the fighting between him and my parents intensified. I tried to steer clear of him. He once refused to get out of bed for school. Our mother threatened to call the police. He didn't move. When the police officer arrived, Cory climbed onto one of the crossbeams in the attic. The officer talked with him, assuring him that she had no jurisdiction to arrest him. She did urge him, though, to cooperate with my parents. He eventually went to school. The conflict didn't end though. He continued to come in and out of the house whenever he wanted to, lashing out at my parents when asked to give information as to his whereabouts.

One Friday afternoon an argument with my mom got particularly intense. My parents had taken away Cory's cell phone and he asked to borrow hers. He had some friends at Crystal Beach (near Galveston) who he wanted to meet up with for the weekend and wanted to coordinate with them. She was not going to let that happen. I could hear the argument in the kitchen from the living room, where my sister and I were watching television. Not wanting to get involved, I sat silently as he loudly berated at her, trying unconvincingly to land his hands on that coveted communication device. She did not back down. Cory, driven by an addict's determination, was not going to let her stop him.

All of a sudden, I heard scuffling in the laundry room. Cory yelled, "Let me see your phone!" My mom shouted back, "Don't touch me!" At that point, I could not stay out of the conflict. My dad was not home to protect my mom, and I had no idea to what extent Cory would go to satisfy his craving.

I jumped up from the living room couch and rushed towards them in the laundry room. The adrenaline was flowing at that point as I sprinted towards him. I had never been in a fight with him, not even engaging in any horseplay with him since we were young children. As I approached him, he backed away from our mom. Instinct took over. I had to do something. From the kitchen countertop, I grabbed a big, thick hardcover book—Cory's *Integrated Physics and Chemistry (IPC)* textbook—and threw it at him. I kept moving towards him, wrestling him to the ground. He tried to swing at my face, his fist just barely touching my cheek—not even enough to leave a bruise. He quickly squirmed away.

Cell phone in hand, he had stormed out of the front door, all the while my sister screaming over and over, "I hate you Cory!" I followed him at a distance of approximately one hundred feet, hoping to get a clue as to where he was going. As he walked toward the neighborhood entrance, he yelled at me to "get the fuck away." He swore that he would kill me for interfering with his drug use. I turned back with shame and resignation when his yelling caught the eye of the neighbor's young toddlers who were playing in the nearby cul-de-sac.

Shaken up, my mom called the police, perhaps more for advice than for any fear of danger for herself. Cory had already run away—her cell phone in hand—for a drugbinging weekend in Galveston. She did not have any desire to press charges against him for simply manhandling a phone from her. The officers did come, however. Going through his belongings with them shed light on the extent of Cory's drug abuse. We uncovered a cannabis plant in his bedroom dresser, a bong made with an ice cream tub, and old ant-farm tubing. "This kid is in deep," one of the officers told my mom.

That night our dad took me to an Al-Anon meeting. I didn't really want to go, but it seemed to be the best option for some immediate form of therapy, which I badly needed at that point. My parents had already begun the twelve-step program for family and loved ones of addicts after Cory was checked into the psychiatric hospital. I didn't quite see a personal value in doing the twelve-step program. It seemed too generic for me. I was willing, nonetheless, to go to a meeting.

We met in a dark, empty schoolhouse building under guise of strict anonymity. Listening to the family members and loved ones of addicts express how deeply wounded they felt, I was moved. After that meeting, I talked with my dad's sponsor, who told me, "it takes a strong man to protect your mother like you did." I cried. I never wanted to be in the position to have to protect my mother from my own brother.

After that night, I moved in with my best friend, Greg. My parents and I agreed that our home was not safe for me while Cory was there. He had repeatedly threatened my life. I would still come home from time to time, though, but only for short periods to gather belongings.

Cory did eventually come home after the weekend. During those rare moments when we crossed paths at home, Cory and I did not speak to each other. My parents told him not to make contact with me.

One day, when I was home collecting a school textbook, however, I happened to see him through a reflection in the mirror in our shared bathroom. He was placing a white paper bag above the towel cabinet. I told my parents.

The next morning in second period theater class, Cory stormed in and pushed me. Arms in air (like a bully pushing on a runt), he exclaimed, "Do you want me to fuck you up?" I tried to talk him down, even if that meant lying. I did not want to re-live another skirmish like the last one, and I definitely did not want our family drama playing out at school, in public view.

"What's wrong?" I responded.

"You know what's wrong!" he snarled, his eyebrows scrunched and his lips curled in anger.

"No seriously, I don't know what you're talking about," I went on somberly, feigning ignorance.

"Then who told mom and dad about the drugs?" he asked, somewhat incredulous of my faked sincerity.

"I don't know. I'm not sure what drugs you mean," I said, putting on the best act possible.

After that exchange, Cory stormed off to the other side of the classroom. Fortunately, that class was in a large room and we seldom had structured activities. Various cliques would form throughout the room and talk for the entire period, so I spent the class on the opposite side of the room from his clique. Not wanting Cory to suspect that I was going to call our parents, I waited until my third period class and begged my teacher to let me use my cell phone (normally not permitted in school) to make an urgent phone call. I told her, in as vague terms as possible, that it had to do with my brother. She could tell from the fear on my face that it was serious. And I knew that she knew our family had been having problems with my brother's drug use. Word had gotten around the grapevine amongst the teachers. "I don't know what's going on at home," she told me, "but I trust that it's an emergency and that you will do the right thing." I walked outside and called our dad from the courtyard in front of the cafeteria, scanning my surroundings for any sign of Cory as I spoke.

"You have to come get him," I said. "He just threatened me in class," I pleaded.

"We're in discussion with the principal's office right now to try to figure out a plan to take him out of school," he said.

"Well somebody has to come do something, because I don't feel safe around him," I continued to desperately plead. I didn't have a plan, but I needed help. I didn't know where they would bring him, but I wanted to be away from him—away from the possibility of any more conflict with him.

My dad arrived within the hour to pick Cory up.

Cory had already walked out of school by the time my dad came. The search didn't last long. The police found him less than a mile down the street, arrested him and brought him to a juvenile detention center with a charge of truancy. He stayed there for a couple of weeks before the judge remanded him to Sundown Ranch, a juvenile drug abuse program set on a farm in rural North Texas. He would spend the last three months of his junior year there, leaving our home quiet during the last three months of my senior year.

After Cory was out of the house, our house became much more tranquil and our lives less stressful. I moved back home from Greg's house, knowing that another major fight with my brother was not going to happen. Moreover, school had become much less demanding. By then, the last cycle had arrived, which did not count towards the final academic rakings. I had finished second in my class and was accepted into my first choice college—Rice University. I was free to spend my evenings playing tennis, going to senior parties, or just resting peacefully on the living room sofa. I could rest assured that I would not come home to conflict. My parents could be confident that Cory was in a drug-free environment.

But life was not back to normal. My friends would ask me where Cory was. I refused to tell them. I would just tell people who asked that he went away and leave it at that. When pressed for more details, I would respond, "I'd rather not discuss it." In part, I was ashamed, but I also feared that his drug buddies would try to contact him if they knew where he was.

Beyond my fear of his retaliation, I felt insecure about my future relationship with Cory. Would he still blame me for being complicit with my parents for forcing him get him off drugs? Would he know that I loved him? In the back of my mind, I worried that we would be estranged once I left for college…. or worse, that he would make good on his earlier threats of revenge.

After a month of no contact with Cory, I finally got to see him. My parents took me to a family weekend at the Sundown Ranch.[i] On a Saturday morning in April, we all woke up early to make the four-hour drive from Beaumont to Canton, Texas. After a two hundred mile ride through the middle-of-nowhere East Texas, we finally pulled into a dirt road, passing llama-filled pastures as we came upon a replica of an old Western town.

Cory was waiting for us outside. He had clearly put on fifteen to twenty pounds, and his buzz-cut had grown out into a scruffy look. He seemed to be much more at peace and deliberate in his movements than when I'd last seen him. When he was on drugs, he was quite jittery and anxious. We shook hands cordially and exchanged small talk before going for lunch in a large dining room in one of the old-West style buildings. We served ourselves from a large buffet of barbeque brisket, potato salad, and baked beans, at ate together, along with another ten to fifteen families, also visiting their adolescents who had come to this place for substance abuse rehabilitation. As we ate, my parents and I kept the conversation topic to descriptive things, such as the food they were feeding him, his contact with the livestock, and opportunities for exercise. We mentioned nothing of his struggle with addiction. Cory was silent for most of the meal, only responding to direct questions. Despite his reticence to communicate, he bore an incredible look of guilt on his face.

A family therapy session followed lunch. It was run by Cory's counselor, Judy, a no-nonsense woman who herself had been through the pits of drug addiction, incarceration and family strife. She grabbed a swivel chair from an adjoining conference room to accommodate the extra people in her office. As we all sat together, Judy started bluntly calling Cory out. She brought up all the hurt that he had caused us. She called his behavior selfish.

He apologized, appearing genuinely penitent. "I am sorry for my behavior," he said. "It was selfish." He was still not crying, though.

Then she brought up the way he treated me. Then she really let loose on Cory. "Look at your brother!" she yelled with sternness that I had never seen anyone show towards him, not even police officers or high school principals.

"Do you want to hurt your brother?!" she hollered, like a drill sergeant hounding a new cadet.

Looking at Cory's face—the somber eyes, raised center eyebrows, quivering lower lip—I could not hold back the tears of hurt.

Judy did not stop.

"You hug him right now!"

He hugged me, gently, and did not let go, something I don't recall him doing since we were toddlers. Then, he, too, began to cry.

"I'm not going to let you off the hook with this one. This is your brother!" she continued. She could sense that he was still holding back his emotions. She wanted to break him—to make him feel the full extent of his guilt for all the pain for which he was responsible.

"Frankly Judy," he replied, "I don't want to be let off the hook."

"I can see it in his face. He loves you and he's going to forgive you, but you've got to apologize for the hurt that you did to him," she said,

Cory did apologize, profusely. He asked forgiveness for all the animosity that he showed me while under the influence of drugs and addiction. I resolved to forgive him. His anger and malice while under the influence of addiction left deep wounds, but I loved him enough to forgive him. He was truly penitent by the look of his eyes.

Still, he was an addict. As Judy reminded us, he would have to struggle with addiction for the rest of his life. The allure of drugs and alcohol would always be too strong for him to learn how to moderate. To love him, she said, meant to love him even when he fell, but never to enable him. When we drank champagne on New Year's, she said, he would have to drink grape juice. Otherwise, if he kept falling into addiction, he would end up in one of three places—jail, institutions or death. He had already been jailed, and he was in an institution now. There was only one other place he could go if he continued to give in to his addiction.

When she said that, I realized the gravity of what Cory was struggling with. Addiction was more than just a bad habit that he couldn't kick. It was a struggle to break free from chains stronger than steel, chains that could suffocate him even when he thought he was free.

Deathly afraid of following down that same path, I foreswore addictive substances. Drinking was not going to happen while I was in college. Even coffee was too risky. I would do anything to keep me from repeating the self-destruction that had consumed my brother.

2.

Breaking Free

"For to be free is not merely to cast off one's chains, but to live in a way that respects and enhances the freedom of others."
—Nelson Mandela

San Diego, California
Wednesday, February 6, 2013

Stepping out of the hotel doors onto the veranda, I felt fresh and energized for the day. I had just had a cup of coffee and breakfast at the hotel. Despite a midnight arrival, I woke up at 7am—just enough time to walk to the prison and arrive by 8:30am.

The view of the San Diego skyline ahead of me helped me get my bearings. The San Diego Bay was directly in front. To the left lie the downtown skyscrapers, one of which was the NBC building Cory had written me about. He could see it from a slit in the wall from his eighth floor cell. Just visually estimating where I lie on the map placed me a couple of miles northeast of the MCC. After a couple of minutes basking in the fresh San Diego morning sun, it was time to walk. My route would take me half a mile to my left and then another half a mile towards the Bay ahead of me. All in all, the trip was just over a mile.

Before heading down the stairs to Seventh Avenue, I pulled out my phone from my pocket and opened the Starbucks app. My hope was to land an espresso between then and the time I got to the MCC. Sure enough there was a Starbucks in the Horton Plaza shopping center—just two blocks east of the MCC. I put my phone into my pocket and head down the stairs to begin my walk.

As I walked along the city sidewalk for the first couple of minutes, the streets seemed unusually quiet. An occasional car passed and a seagull or two squawked, but the city seemed to be still asleep. For a second I thought as if it wasn't a city at all. The quietness was the opposite of what I am used to in a city.

But then, as I neared Broadway Street—the nucleus of downtown—the silence disappeared. The trolley on Broadway Street rang its bell. Pedestrian traffic picked up. Taxis filled the street. Businesses picked up as usual. For a few minutes, however, the metropolitan center was quiet.

I probably wouldn't have even remembered the silence had it not reminded me of being a pilgrim on the Way of Saint James, or El Camino de Santiago. Having walked the Way before, I was quite familiar with the unease that many pilgrims feel when coming to a large city. Cities would always come as a shock to the stillness to which pilgrims accustom when walking most days along rural farmlands and uninhabited forests. There is something unnatural about the hustle of activity in our modern cities that the pilgrim becomes acutely aware of.

As a pilgrim, the only way for me to stay calm in the city was to savor those moments of serenity that are all-too-easily passed by in my usual city life: the shade of a tree in a city park, the coastal breeze running through my hair, the chirp of sparrows hopping around in search of food and those moments of silence when walking through a city street on a fresh, sunny morning.

It was in search of moments of silence like these that was a motivation for me to walk the Way the first time some four years prior. I was living in New York at the time, and the noise of city life had become difficult to bear. Growing up in the South, I was not used to hearing outside my bedroom window taxis honking, police sirens blazing or news helicopters hovering. There were of course hidden alcoves where I could find relative silence—a hidden trail near 92nd street in Central Park, Roosevelt Island across the East River, and the Cloister near Inman Park. Even those places were becoming difficult to appreciate, however, amidst my distractedness. As my first year of medical school progressed, I kept finding excuses to distract myself from a mental break. There was always something to study.

I almost in fact didn't even go on the Way. While planning our honeymoon, I had suggested to my wife (then fiancée) that we skip the Way and I spend the summer doing research for medical school. We could still spend a couple of weeks traveling to Spain or Latin America, I mentioned. She insisted, however, that we go on the Way. It was indeed our dream. The Way was too important for us to forego, she said. Besides, I needed a break from city life, she said. The anxiety was getting to me. I was sleeping poorly and beginning to feel depressed. This was the only Way to recover. She was not about to let me forget our resolution that we had made when we first started dating in college. We had agreed that should we get married, and we would walk the Way of Saint James for our honeymoon.

We had learned about the Way from a poster.[ii] I had hung it on my door in my dorm room. The poster, which depicted various churches from along the Way, was given to me by a professor of Hispanic Studies[iii] (my college major). We had been studying in his class the age of Queen Isabella and King Ferdinand—two major supporters of infrastructure along the Way.

The Way was of particular interest to both of us. Having met at the college Spanish table, we had both become fluent in Spanish, and we both were recent Catholic converts. So, after our honeymoon we left immediately from Houston to Europe, where we began the French Way from the Pyrenees. We walked a total of nearly 1100 kilometers (700 miles) to get to Santiago, beginning in the town of Lourdes.

Along the Way, we found as honeymooners, more than just an opportunity to learn Spanish history or improve our fluency. We found a connection to a part of ourselves that we simply didn't make in our pre-pilgrim lives. The noise of city life was replaced with the silence of natural landscapes along the Pyrenees, La Rioja,

Castilla or Galicia. Distraction with the thought of 'what-to do-next' was replaced with the steady rhythm of a pilgrim's day. Get up early, walk, find a place to eat breakfast and lunch, find a place to eat, shower, do laundry, eat dinner and sleep. That is the basic rhythm of a pilgrim's life. Nothing else has to be done. With this rhythm came a certain reflectiveness. The everyday things I was doing in haste—eating, doing laundry, even talking to others—suddenly became more deliberate and meaningful. I was living a much happier life than as a medical student. I was even sleeping well. No longer did I feel anxious to always do something.

It was during our honeymoon that I began drinking coffee again. There café was just part of the breakfast routine along with bread, butter and jam. Drinking a cup of espresso then became a morning routine that I continued throughout medical school. Never once did I use it to stay up to study.

***

After crossing Front Street, I glanced around the small park for a trashcan to throw away my empty Starbucks cup. I had been fortunate enough to locate the Starbucks I was looking for. The double shot was just what I wanted. After throwing the cup away, I walked towards the MCC building, which lie just in front of me. As I neared the MCC, passing the park benches seated along the walkway, a young man in a buzz cut in a grey jumpsuit sat on one of the benches writing in a journal. I nearly passed him. It did not appear at first sight to be my brother. He looked too slim and young to be my brother—a high school version of him. I hadn't seen him in a buzz cut since then. Just to make sure, I said his name.

"Cory?"

He looked up. It was him indeed. He was slower and more deliberate in his movements than I had ever seen him. Beside him were a large cardboard box, a small, black backpack and a black trash-bag. He set down his journal and got up to hug me.

"Yo, brother," I said. We embraced.

"Thanks for coming," he said.

"Glad I was free to help," I said.

I looked beside him at a cardboard box sitting next to him, filled mostly with books. I was not about to lug that across Downtown San Diego, much less on a plane with a connecting flight through LAX.

"Well," I said, "Why don't we see if we can mail some of your stuff so we don't have to carry it on the plane?"

He seemed uneasy with me asking his input on practical arrangements. He just went along. I picked up the box and carried it for him. We walked towards Market Street on Front Street. I had seen from my online searching the day before that there were several shipping centers near there.

"How's it going?" I asked as we walked, not wanting to be too blunt about the fact of his recent 12-month prison sentence. He seemed quite blasé.

"I just got a laugh out of the security guards when they saw me walking out of the entrance in street clothes. They looked at me puzzled, like, is he supposed to be there?"

I chuckled.

The first shipping store we found was closed until 9am. It was 8:30am at the time. The second one we found was—according to the sign in front—also closed. We tried opening the doors. They were open and a woman standing at the counter told us that she would open soon. We waited outside the door until she opened. Looking at the freight that I was carrying, she beckoned us in early. The box that Cory stored his books in was open and nearly falling apart, so we searched the store for a sturdy box that would fit them.

We found a large box and began to pack his belongings into the box. I suggested we throw away or recycle some books that seemed quite ragged, but he insisted on keeping all of them.

"They are very important to me—my only real possessions," he said. He had spent the majority of his time in prison reading and writing. Per his request, friends and family would send him books via Amazon—the only allowed book sender. One of those books that I recently sent him was 'Seven Tips to Make the Most of

Santiago de Compostela.' He read it and immediately wrote me about it:

September 29, 2012
Dear Landon,
Thank you kindly for the books. I received 'Seven Tips to Make the Most of Santiago de Compostela' and 'The Portal to the Mystery of Hope' yesterday in the mail. I'm halfway through the second and read the first this morning. In what I would later deem to be arrogance, I flipped hastily through the book thinking 'Ha, what could this amateur tell ME about enduring a mere month of living out of a backpack.' But today, as I read, I became thoroughly captivated, because even if it's a very novice guide, just entertaining the ideas of the pilgrimage was a joy. I am and have been convinced I would enjoy/appreciate it (the pilgrimage), even if, on my own, I would prioritize a few other tracks before it... Varanagi, Bodhgaya, Appalachian. Given an opportunity to make the trip or part of it with you, I will do it....

I had proposed walking the Way together after finding out that his release date would correspond with my month-long vacation prior to graduating from medical school. He and I had not seen each other since he was imprisoned, and we had spent little time together since our early teens. Though we had reconciled over trauma he inflicted in high school while on drugs, our lives continued to diverge once I moved away from home. The Way of Saint James seemed to be the perfect trip to bring our lives together. It had everything we could hope for in a brother-brother bonding experience: outdoors, meditation, historical learning, and most of all, simplicity.

After repackaging the books in a sturdier box, the

woman at the counter rung up the shipping options. Best option was ground delivery via UPS. Cost was about $100. Cory grabbed a wad of crisp cash an envelope he had carried with him without bothering to count out the total. The manager looked perplexed that he wasn't counting out the money. I helped Cory count out the total. We paid and left the packaging center for our walk back to the hotel, where I had left my bag. Our flight departed at lunchtime.

As we left the store, the thought crossed my mind to ask him in person about the book. This would be a perfect segway into concrete planning for the trip, which would have to happen soon if we were going to walk it in April—the other month I had for vacation from medical school. We had much more to discuss about walking the Way if it were going to be more than just an idea.

That discussion would have to wait however, until we figured out where we were going. After exiting the store, we walked to the corner of the street and stopped. We had to figure out which turn to take. Cory just looked at me. He wasn't the least bit interested in taking the lead on directions. I looked at my watch. Not even 9am. We had several hours before the flight.

"We have some time. Do you want to walk to the hotel or take a taxi?"

"Let's walk," he said, "...if we have time."

We continued to walk north, away from the packaging store and the MCC. As we walked, we continued to talk about the surprised look of the prison guard's face when Cory walked out the front door. This led to a discussion about prison guards. Many of them, he said, appeared frustrated with their jobs. They were often times honest, hard-working guards, he said, who found themselves in a position of enforcing confinement of convicts they knew didn't need to be there. Some, he said, needed to be there, he said, but others were non-violent offenders in for minor drug offenses who faced hefty sentences due to harsh sentencing laws.

I looked straight ahead and mulled over what he said. I tried to think about his comments with a detached, cerebral poise as possible. It was the only way I could keep from letting my emotions show. Though I knew he had become the most pacifist, peace-filled convict to be released from prison that day, memories of our past lay at the forefront of my mind. Fear of conflict to the point of violence could easily take hold of my feelings.

As we passed the Cathedral of Saint Joseph, we could see our hotel lying above the hill. I asked Cory if he wanted to get breakfast at the buffet before it closed. He declined the offer but asked for a change of clothes. He wanted to discard the jumpsuit gifted to him by the prison system, he said. It felt entirely too hot. We entered the hotel lobby, passing the veranda en route to my room. In our corner hotel room, I grabbed from my backpack a pair of jeans, a long-sleeve tee shirt and my old walking shoes.

"I'll meet you in the breakfast room," I told him, as I handed him the clothes.

I headed down to the breakfast lounge. In the lounge, I found a table next to the window, sat down and pulled out my journal. I grabbed my pen and wrote: *6 Feb 2013, HI Express Downtown San Diego.* I stopped. So much had happened in the past 24 hours that I didn't even know where to begin. Hoping to take a few minutes to compose my thoughts, I gazed outside the window to the street, Seventh Avenue. My attention began to wander, however, as the Fox News Bell sounded on the TV screens overhead.[iv] I finally turned my gaze back to my journal, struggling to focus my attention for a few minutes. I jotted down a few events from the past morning. They weren't detailed—just enough to remind myself of details I would otherwise forget…The blaring Fox News bell, the tattered box Cory had stored his books in, the grey jumpsuit Cory wore when I found Cory on the park bench…

Cory came into the breakfast room and sat across from me, throwing his black daypack stuffed with his grey jumpsuit onto the chair beside him.

"Are you sure you don't want anything to eat?" I asked again.

"No," he said. "I'm trying something called alternate day fasting. Have you heard of it?"

"No," I said.

He explained to me his strategy of "alternate day fasting." It basically boiled down to every other day fasting, which he claimed was more reflective of the diet of our Paleolithic ancestors. This was how he managed to stay thin in prison, he noted.

"Hmm," I said, in response to his explanation, nodding with as little look of judgment on my face as possible. I didn't disbelieve him, per se. Every other day fasting seemed quite excessive, however. If it worked for him, though, I was not about to judge him.

"Well, if you're not going to eat, we should probably get to the airport," I said. Our flight left at noon, and by that time it was 10am. He followed me to the lobby where I asked a taxi to be called. Cory stopped me before leaving the desk.

"We can just take a bus," he said.

"We should just play it safe," I countered. I did not want to have travel plans interrupted to figure out bus route logistics. I didn't want to disagree with him, but I had in the back of my mind a worry that his name might show up on a black list of travelers not allowed to fly. He was, after all, a convict. Cory was, undoubtedly, concerned about cost. He never liked to spend money. The hotel desk clerk looked at us both, waiting for a decision. Were Cory in high school, he would have insisted on his own route, regardless of whether I went with him, but he had mellowed out in prison.

"Oh," Cory said, leaving the issue at that. We went along with the taxi reservation.

Taxi arrangements made, we went back to the room where quickly I packed my backpack and scurried back to the lobby. Whilst we waited, Cory and I walked onto the veranda. The morning sun had come up. The air was still crisp. I asked Cory to pose in front of the San Diego skyline. Friends and family would appreciate seeing him free and well. He seemed uneasy. He sheepishly went down the stairs to the lower level of the veranda, while I took a photo from the stairs above. I told him to wait while I beckoned someone from the lobby to take a photo of both of us, but the taxi driver pulled up. Afterwards, I quickly grabbed my backpack and we headed down to the airport.

We sat silently in the cab. Neither of us had any desire to explain to the cab driver the circumstances that brought us from San Diego. As we sat, the opportunity seemed ideal to bring up my proposal to walk the Camino. We had only corresponded in writing about it once back in September. I did not want to overwhelm him, though. Still, I did not want to put off the conversation until we got back to Houston. Then he would be immersed in the drama of reuniting with my parents and meeting Benny for the first time, after which point my parents would bring him to the halfway house in San Antonio. His communication there would be restricted for several weeks. I was scheduled to leave for London within a couple of weeks for a month-long rotation with the National Health Service (NHS). Communicating with Cory from Europe would be difficult. I thought for a couple of minutes how to bring up the subject, but within five minutes the taxi had pulled onto North Harbor drive from which the airport was in sight. The conversation would have to wait until later.

We arrived at the airport with well over an hour before boarding—much sooner than expected. It didn't take long for Cory to pass security. With the extra time I brought Cory to the United lounge. We were certainly not first class travelers, but I had accumulated a handful of those ubiquitous passes that come with annual credit card rewards. Cory followed along silently.

When we got there, he seemed uncomfortable as he surveyed the layout—clean tables, a snack bar, leather couches. He did not expect to partake of such comfort after the meagerness of living in prison. "How much do I owe you?" he asked. I assured him the passes were free. He followed me along as we found a perch to rest our backpacks in a corner near a window overlooking the runway. When we sat down, it occurred to me that we hadn't called my mother. I called, assuring her that the pickup went smooth. She asked to speak to Cory. I handed the phone to him.

As he spoke I went to the snack bar to get another espresso. When I came back, Cory had finished talking to my mom. He handed me the phone. We sat for a while, making only small talk about the lounge and the trip to the airport. He still seemed uneasy with the lounge. After half an hour, it was time for us to make it to the gate.

We made our way to the gate and boarded without incident. By my own doing, Cory and I sat together on both flights. We had a connecting flight through LAX to take us to Houston. After we settled into our seats, I introduced the subject of traveling to Cory, talking about lifetime trips that he might like to take. He mentioned a pilgrimage in the Himalayas. I asked him what he thought about New Zealand. He said he would enjoy it but was barred from the Country as a convicted criminal. We continued to talk about different travel destinations we might like to visit. Growing up in Texas, we had not traveled outside the US as children except to go across the border to Mexico a couple of times. Though I had traveled many times to Europe during my years in medical school, Cory and I had not traveled outside the country together apart from Mexico.

After a few minutes, I just blurted out the question.

"So what do you think about the idea of walking the Camino?" He looked out the window and paused for a moment.

"I like the idea. I mean, I don't know much about it…other than what the book you sent me says. It sounds great. I just need to keep expenses at a minimum."

"This would only take up a fraction of the settlement," I responded.

While in prison, Cory had been plaintiff in a personal injury lawsuit prior to being incarcerated. An unsuspecting car driver hit him while on a bike ride. Given that he had the right of way, the driver was deemed at fault. He settled on $50,000 several months before being released.

"If you're worried about expenses, this shouldn't cost too much," I added. "After the plane flight, we're just talking about food and albergues," I said.

"What are albergues?" he asked.

I explained to him the concept of *albergues*—hostels along the Way.[v] Typically set up by volunteers to provide low-cost accommodations to pilgrims, I continued.

"Hmm," he said. He kept silent for a moment, looking out the airplane window. Bringing up such an adventure so soon, I could tell, was a bit much for him to contemplate. Still, I didn't want to lose the chance to have this talk in person. He turned back towards me and nodded.

"Given the fact that this is something you know about, and it is with you, I'm willing."

At that we were silent for a moment. I looked at my phone: 2pm. Over twenty-four hours had passed since I heard about Cory's release and booked the flight from Houston. We were now en route to return to Texas. After a few minutes, Cory changed the subject to my son Benny, whom he was looking forward to meeting. We left our discussion of Camino plans for another time.

3.

A Wrench (Or Two) In The Plans

The best laid schemes o' Mice an' Men
Gang aft agley,
An' lea'e us nought but grief an' pain,
For promis'd joy!
—Robert Burns, 'To a Mouse'

Telegraph Hill, London, United Kingdom
March 7, 2013

Just as I walked in the door, I threw my backpack down on the bed and sat at the simple, wooden school desk nestled in the corner of my bedroom. I was in London, working as a medical student at an inner city General Practice near Waterloo Station. Cory and I had planned an afternoon Skype. After a month in the halfway house, he had been released. I grabbed my phone to call Cory.

We had settled the question of whether we would go on the Camino together. Our departure date would be April 16. That behind us, I wanted to touch base with him about how best to get to Saint Jean Pied de Port—the traditional starting point of the French Way—which was the major route most pilgrims take. I was hoping that we could agree on getting to Pamplona via train or plane, from which we could take a bus to Saint Jean.

When I reached Cory, his concerns ran deeper than logistics. As soon as our Skype calls connected, he sounded distressed.

“I'm feeling kind of upset with myself,” he relayed.

I stood up from where I was seated on the bed, bracing myself for what he would say.

“Why, what's wrong?” I asked.

“So first, Corey asked me to loan him $5,000 to help pay for a new lawyer,” he begins. Corey was his best friend who he met while in jail in Louisiana. Corey was still in jail. This was not going to be good news. He continued—“then I have this other friend who doesn’t work and owes a lot of money. When he found out I got the settlement, he asked me for some money. When I told him I would loan it to him, he’s just like, ‘how ‘bout another thousand for this, or can you give me another thousand for this, or another thousand for that?’ In the end, I caved.”

“How much did you give him?” I asked, staring out the window of the bedroom.

“Entirely too much,” he repeated, clearly not wanting to tell.

"Let's just say that I'm going to have to minimize costs on the Camino because everything I'm going to need to spend there I'm going to have to work for between now and then."

"Is there any way you can get him to pay you back—even some of it—before you leave?" I asked.

"I can try, but I don't think I'm going to get a penny back. He doesn't work and is not very trustworthy. I'm just feeling so bad about letting myself get talked into it. He just kept bringing up more and more reasons he needed money. In the end, I gave him entirely too much."

"Well, look," I said, trying to sound as conciliatory as possible, "What's done is done. The best we can do is work with what you have. Should you get into a bind before the trip, you know that Amanda and I will help you."

"I really appreciate that, but I don't want to have to ask you guys for money. I just need to know, what's the minimum amount I need to get by? Because I'm going to have to earn almost all of it before we leave."

I paused for a second. Phone in hand, I gazed out the window. Again, as when we were walking from prison to the hotel, I tried to think as cerebrally as possible, not letting my feelings get the best of me.

"Well, the flights are already paid for," I said. My mom had already deducted the cost of the flights from his settlement and reimbursed me. "All you really need to pay for now is food and shelter, and public albergues are pretty inexpensive—no more than 6 Euros. If you want you can always buy groceries and avoid restaurants. Maybe ten Euros per day would be for food. So total expenses—if you're really frugal—should be about 16 Euros a day. This is about $20, so multiply that times 30 days. You shouldn't need more than $600."

"Add to that transportation to get to and from Madrid and we're talking no more than $1000. That shouldn't be so hard to earn over a month."

"You don't understand. I hardly have a penny, so I don't just need to earn that. I need to earn enough to live on before…and to not be penniless when I get back…"

His voice trailed off for a few seconds.

"I'm just really upset with myself about all this. I just let myself get duped."

"Don't beat yourself up over this." I interjected, "The best we can do is work with what we've got." I said. "Why don't we get in touch later once I've done some more research on travel plans?"

"Okay," he said.

I hung up the phone, incredulous over conversation that had just taken place. While in prison, Cory was awarded more money than Amanda and I ever had in our possession. Not three weeks out of the halfway house, he hardly had a penny in his pocket. I did not know what to think. I continued to stare out the window after I hung up. The grey skies and steady drizzle masked the otherwise picturesque view of Victorian homes lining the street. Was this darkness an omen? I did not want to think so.

I turned my thoughts elsewhere. The most pressing concern for me at the moment was warming the tips of my toes, which were nippy. Heating during an unusually cold March had been a challenge in the old Victorian home. I grabbed a copy of *The Hobbit* from my desk and headed upstairs to the bathroom.

As the bath water ran, I gazed out the window Victorian houses across the street. This time, I was high enough to see behind them a panorama of the London skyline. To one side stood the Gherkin, a torpedo shaped skyscraper in the heart of the financial district; to the other the Shard of Glass, an 87-story glass paned edifice above London Bridge. I feared that the Shard might be an omen for our pilgrimage. Our best-laid plans seemed to be breaking into shards. Cory, in his penitent but naïve post-convict life had not kept his finances together enough to pay for this trip we had been planning, funds he'd had a few weeks before. His heart had become too soft to hold onto money.

I felt angry and annoyed with him for his lack of good judgment. I wanted him to consider his choices with more equanimity. I wanted him to see that not all giving to others was good—especially when he was being hurt or taken advantage of. Simply put, he had risked letting our trip fall through the cracks.

These feelings of irritation were soon overshadowed by empathy and hope. This pilgrimage could help rebuild our brotherly bond and perhaps help Cory become more grounded. Despite supporting a new baby, residency moving expenses and Amanda's meager income as a first-year teacher, I felt the need to help him go on this trip. I knew that Cory had a sense of compassion, albeit a misplaced one. Now he was cash strapped before even setting foot out of the door.

The bath was nearly full when I looked back. I grabbed *The Hobbit* and lay down in the tub to read.

"Chapter 1: An Unexpected Party"…

Reading about Bilbo's unexpected party of dwarves—I hoped—would get me in the JRR Tolkien spirit. Hobbits are simple creatures, content to live their lives enjoying creature comforts in their little homes on the shire. Worrying about next week's plans would be unheard of for a hobbit when so much was available to enjoy at present. As the bath water warmed my toes, I tried to get into the mind-frame of a hobbit, allowing, for the moment, the luxury of the present to prevail over next month's plans, its complications, for the moment.

***

New York City, the Avalon (Morningside Park)

April 9, 2013

I was in New York City for a couple of weeks to take a medical school course. The gargoyles of the Cathedral of St John the Divine were just barely visible at dawn. As I waited on hold, I tried to trace out the contours of one of the gargoyles. United Airlines was on the line. I was waiting to speak to a customer service representative. Estimated wait time: 30 minutes. Yet the wait was necessary—I had to talk with someone about getting Cory's and my flight changed.

Otherwise, I risked leaving our family homeless when I returned from the Way. Two weeks after my return, our lease in Houston would expire and my internship in Cambridge was set to begin in June. We needed to find a place to live. Amanda and I made a trip to Cambridge the previous weekend to find an apartment, but we had been unable to secure housing during our trip. We learned then that Cambridge was one of the most competitive markets in the Boston area. In order to find an apartment, I had no choice other than to delay our departure. I had called Cory earlier in the day to propose this itinerary change, to which he agreed.

An agent answered after another half-hour on hold staring at the gargoyles.

"Thank you for calling United, how may I assist you!" she cheerily asked in a Filipino accent.

I explained to her why I needed to change the flight: to find a place to live for our family. She put me on hold for a few minutes then came back on-line and said that she would gladly make the change for a fee of $500. For Amanda and me, this extra expense was substantial, and we would pay for Cory and me both, as Cory had no extra funds to spare.

I pled with the agent to waive the fee. I tried sharing all of the circumstances with my brother up to that point: my decade-long estrangement with my brother, and our need for this trip together. I hoped I would find in her a sympathetic ear towards our plight. She stood firm, however, insisting that we pay the fee for any change. I felt sorely disappointed. Any change would cost us even more.

Facing this additional cost, I planned to cancel the trip. Earlier in the day, when Cory learned that Amanda and I had not been able to find an apartment, he suggested that we cancel their trip. While he was still willing to go, he suggested that we postpone it for a more convenient time in life. We agreed to go ahead with the travel plans, moreover, provided that I could arrange for a flight change.

I called Amanda. Nudging with support, she reminded me that there would be no other time in the foreseeable future when we would have this opportunity. I would never be able to get a month off from residency to make a pilgrimage. Even if I did get time off, our son Benny would be too old for me to be away from him for long. The older he gets, she said, the more he would need me nearby every day.

Despite her cogent reasoning, I was still hesitant to go forward with travel plans. I did not want to spend any more time or money on this trip.

"We could just schedule a trip nearby couldn't we?" I suggested.

"What about the Appalachians, or California? That would give us a chance to just be out in nature and reconnect," I continued.

"It's not the same," Amanda stated firmly.

"Why do you say that?" I asked.

"You know that you and I were different after we walked the Camino," she said. She then elaborated, reminding me that the *Camino* could not be replicated anywhere else—the churches, the fraternity with other pilgrims, the closeness to history…all in addition to the nature and simplicity.

"This is more than just some nature hike," she went on. "This is about you and Cory connecting over something deeper."

I listened intently as she talked. She was right, and I knew it…even before I asked her. But I wanted her to remind me why the *Camino* was the right path for us. In my weakness, I was tempted to overlook the reasons why I had asked Cory to go with me.

"The right thing to do is clear," she said. "This is what

you and your brother need," she said, "and if it cost an extra $500, we'll make it work."

Armed with her support and encouragement, I pulled out my laptop, logged on to the United website and made the flight change. We would leave one week later: on April 22. This would give us another week to find housing in Cambridge. Our trip would be cut short, as I had to be back in New York on May 10 for a final class in medical school required of all graduating seniors. We would have 18 days to walk the Way, which would not be nearly enough to walk from Saint Jean Pied de Port, even if we were fast walkers. We would have to alter our route, but I would have to work on planning that route later. My immediate concern was house hunting.

***

Somerville, MA
Thursday April 18, 2013

The skies were blue and the sun bright as I began a morning run down Somerville Avenue. I stopped briefly at Starbucks hoping to get an espresso. The door was locked. I stood a few moments in front of the sign, at first perturbed. While I had heard on the morning news that the suspects for the Boston Marathon bombing were on the loose in the area after exchanging gunfire with an MIT officer in Kendall Square, I had not heard anything about businesses in the city being shut down.

I continued on my run. When I noticed that other storefronts were also shut down, I turned back to Davis Square, where I had reserved a room with a family via AirBnB. I wasn't worried about getting in the middle of terrorist crossfire, which was not very likely, but I figured if Starbucks was closed, who knew whether flights from Logan would be in operation? I quickly made it back to the house.

After a quick shower, I packed my backpack and made my way Davis Square to catch the MBTA to the airport. The sooner I could get to the airport, the more likely my chances were to catch a flight. But the MBTA had shut down for the day. The doors at the Davis Square stop were completely locked. Fortunately, however, a lone taxi was parked outside CVS. The driver agreed to take me to the airport.

I jumped into the cab, sat in the back, buckled my seat belt, and let out a huge sigh of relief. The past week had been hectic enough. After moving our flights back a week, I promised not to return until I secured an apartment lease in Cambridge. Fortunately, I found a place that we could afford and had submitted an application the night before.

Glancing at my backpack beside me in the backseat of the cab, I recalled that our flight to Madrid was in four days. I had not thought about the Way since making our flight changes the week prior. I would have to dig up my hiking backpacks from the closet and pack them over the weekend. I would use one, Cory, the other. I would also have to figure out which route we would take to

Santiago. With a medical school and the apartment search the week prior, I had no time to plan anything more than our flight change. It was Thursday. I would have to plan our route when I got home to Houston, provided I made it back in time.

The flights from Boston's Logan Airport could very well have been grounded. I did not know at the time.

As we turned into the terminal access road, we came to a rolling stop. Ahead was bumper-to-bumper traffic. Armed National Guardsmen were posted at each side of the highway. After ten minutes of stop-and-go traffic, we finally reached the checkpoint, where Massachusetts State Troopers checked our trunk before sending us along. The taxi dropped me off at the terminal, where travelers freely entered and exited the terminal entry doors. After going through security, I checked the departure screens. My flight was still scheduled to depart on time. I breathed a sigh of relief. At least some things were business as usual.

***

Houston, TX
Friday April 19, 2013

Benny had just fallen asleep in his crib for his mid-morning nap, which would give me at least an hour of quiet time. As I sat at the desk, I watched him as he slept. His tiny little arms sprawled out. Rhythmically, he breathed. I loved to just watch him breathe. Did I really want to leave him? The thought of being away from him for more than a few days was tough to swallow.

After the feat of having to find an apartment in Cambridge and the fiasco of getting to the airport, I had no time to make any further plans. Well rested and back at our home in Houston, this was my chance to plan our route. I pulled up Google Maps on my computer. After locating Santiago de Compostela, I zoomed out until the whole Iberian Peninsula took up the screen. I routed Saint Jean Pied de Port to Santiago: 782 km via highway A6. This would require walking between 48 and 52 kilometers per day to get to Santiago. Impossible. That's 30 miles per day. If we did not drop dead from exhaustion, we would certainly lack in quality time.

Searching for an alternative route, I pulled out our *credenciales* that I had ordered from the American pilgrim's association—American Pilgrims on the Camino. *Credenciales*, or credentials, are passports that pilgrims are required to carry as proof of pilgrimage. They must be presented to each albergue, where they will be stamped with a unique emblem. At the end of the pilgrimage, the stamps serve as a record of where the pilgrim has stayed and as proof of one's journey when presented to the Office of Pilgrims at the Cathedral of Santiago. On the back of the credential is a map off different routes to Santiago from within Europe.

Scanning the map of different starting points on the Iberian Peninsula, the next best option would have to be somewhere closer to Santiago. León was one possibility. I pulled up Google Maps and mapped León to Santiago:

319kilometers (200 miles). This would make our daily walk approximately 21 kilometers (13 miles)—much more within reason. Even so, this route made me uneasy. As the number of pilgrims walking the Way has increased over recent years, the last several hundred kilometers were becoming more and more tourist-like, as Amanda and I experienced when we went.[vi] This would be less than ideal. Cory and I needed to be alone together and not amid tourist crowds.

I pulled out my credential again and scanned it in earnest, looking for a starting point for our pilgrimage. Just above León was Oviedo. I knew about the coastal town from its description by a *hospitalero*. *Hospitaleros* are volunteers—usually from the nearby community—who maintain *albergues* along the Way. They usually spend a few hours a day, welcoming pilgrims, stamping credentials, and collecting *donativos*—small donations (usually between 5 and 10 Euros, $6 and $12) requested of pilgrims for upkeep. The *hospitalero* who told us about Oviedo was Inyaku—Basque for Ignatius. He ran the albergue in Irun, a coastal town on the border with France just outside of San Sebastián. Inyaku was a volunteer there for most of the season when he wasn't walking the Way himself. (He had walked it 17 times.) When we'd met Inyaku, he told us that we had to stop by Oviedo. As the proverb went:

Quien pasa por el Camino y no visita al Salvador [the Cathedral in Oviedo]

Visita al criado y deja al señor.

"He who goes on the Way and does not visit the Savior [the Cathedral in Oviedo]

Visits the servant but leaves behind his lord."

We didn't heed his words at the time. Instead, we hiked into Galicia going through León—the traditional French Way. On my return from Spain, I'd vowed to visit Oviedo the next time I walked the Way.

Inyaku's words in mind, I routed the distance from Oviedo to Santiago: 339km. Similar to the distance from León. I pulled up a map of the Primitive Way on another browser tab and tried to compare it to the driving route. Google Maps was unable to provide any driving or biking routes along the Primitive Way. In fact, there were no major cities from Oviedo to Lugo on the Primitive Way—about 200km of the trip. Scanning the Google maps route, I pulled up the topographical view. Mostly mountains along the Primitive Way.

I tried calling Cory to discuss the options. He didn't answer. He was surely busy working to earn money for the trip. Earlier in the week, I had mentioned that walking the entire Way might not be possible given our time limits. He had given me license to "do what you think is best." I considered waiting for a return call, but that could be days. Cory was known to be erratic in his call patterns. Cory was, moreover, completely at ease with last minute arrangements. I, on the other hand was not comfortable leaving the trip's details until the last minute. I tried to think of what he would most enjoy, envisioning the options before us—the more traveled, more comfortable and more tourist-trodden path, or the less traveled, rugged path, rightly called the Primitive Way. In that moment, only one seemed right—going off the beaten path.

I picked up my phone to call Iberia Airlines and book our flights to Oviedo.

***

Houston, TX
April 21, 2013

It was the morning we were scheduled to depart Houston for Spain when my mom whispered to me "Cory never came home," as I lay asleep in bed.

"What?" I moaned with my eyes wide shut. I had been in a deep sleep when she came into my bedroom. Amanda had already left for work. Benny lay asleep in the crib next to me.

"He never came home last night," repeated my mom. I opened my eyes and turned towards her.

"Did you call him?" I responded.

"He's not answering. He was supposed to drive here after work."

"Well, we'll see if he shows up," I said. She left the room. I buried my head into my pillow and tried in earnest to fall back asleep.

Arriving at last minute was a classic Cory move, I told myself. He had promised that he would make the drive from Austin to arrive a day before our departure, and if he didn't make it, he probably had good reason. I believed he would come. Still, doubts crossed my mind after my mother tried to wake me with concern. What if he got in a car wreck on the way here? Or what if he fell back into drugs and was hung over? I tossed and turned in bed, as I tried to distract myself from worrying about him. I tried to envision the day's itinerary, what I needed to pack, and last minute information that needed to be printed out. I tried occupying my mind with anything that might block me from thinking about any number of horrible scenarios, yearning for release from the Pandora's box my mom announcement had opened. But the thoughts just kept cropping up, though, like a thick tar seeping out of the box and sticking to everything it touches.

Restless, I climbed out of bed, donned my bathrobe and walked to the kitchen to make coffee. My mom sat in the living room. In the following weeks, my mom, my sister and Amanda's father, "Team Benny"—as Cory called them—would help care for my son Benny. My wife, who unselfishly encouraged this trip, and Team Benny were our only hope for making this pilgrimage being possible. I looked out from the kitchen and noted that my mom was peering out the front window—every few minutes—hoping to see Cory walking up the path to our front door.

***

Victoria, TX
May 2005

Mom paced around the living room, stopping to peer out the window next to the front door of our house in Victoria. Her face bore a look that alternated between fear and hope. She kept looking at an empty driveway with no sign of Cory's Toyota minivan. It was nearly midnight of graduation night and he was not at home. It was not unusual for him to be out with friends, but how late he had been coming back recently gave my mom concern. There had been other signs to raise concern, but I didn't know about them. Nobody wanted to mention the elephant in the room: Cory was back on drugs. He had sobered up after his three-month stay at Sundown Ranch. After that, our family underwent some major changes. I had left home for college. Mom, Dad, Cory and Bethany moved from Beaumont to Victoria, Texas, some four hours away. With this move, Cory spent his senior year of high school at a different school than the one he had been attending when he first began using drugs.

"Still not back yet," mom said, walking from the window to the living room. Our maternal grandmother, Meime, was standing in the living room, noted my mother's concern. She was never afraid of being blunt.

"I think that Cory might be using again," she said.

Mom took a deep breath. She said nothing, retreating back into her bedroom. Seated at the kitchen table just next to the living room, I stood up from my chair. I headed to my bedroom in the garage apartment upstairs.

That conversation was over. Nobody in our family wanted to open that box. If Cory were using drugs, we all felt that we were better off not knowing about it. Especially for me, I didn't want to know if he had relapsed. Even though he apologized at Sundown Ranch the previous year, the memories of hurt were deep. I was not about to be present when he arrived, risking the possibility of bearing witness to conflict with my parents. To expose myself to even the possibility of conflict with him over drugs would be like handling bleach with an open wound on my hand. The risk of tearing into wounds and creating a deeper scar was simply too much for me.

"Okay," my grandmother said, calmly as possible. "I guess I will go to bed too."

My grandmother was the only one brave enough to be blunt. Even if she knew about his drug use, she did not experience the visceral reaction on hearing the words "Cory" and "drugs" in the same sentence. She had not been present for the previous year's drama as those who lived with him had. The possibility of Cory using drugs was a subject that none of us wanted to broach.

***

Houston, TX
April 21, 2013

After being woken up over Cory's no-show, I left my house to buy hiking shoes. My mom stayed home and took care of Benny. As I drove to the sporting goods outlet, rain began to fall. The thought of Cory not showing up crossed my mind, but I distracted myself. I was still going to plan as if we were going. I turned my thoughts to what I needed to be prepared for the Asturian Mountains. Seeing the rain drops on my car, I realized that I needed a rain poncho.

As I was driving home, Cory showed up. He had worked late into the evening at a construction job that took more time than expected. Growing too tired to drive home late at night, he had parked, sleeping in his car until morning. He was now sleeping on our couch.

While I was relieved to hear that Cory was well and had finally arrived, I felt annoyed. He did not so much as have the courtesy to call us to let us know that he would not be arriving the night before—as planned. I had to put aside my annoyance though. Cory stayed out trying to earn money for this trip, and he didn't even have a cell phone with which to call me. He was trying to earn money so he didn't have to ask me for help should he run out. I couldn't fault him for his good will, even if he made me worry. I was relieved, most of all, that we had passed the roadblocks in our way to walk the Way together, after years of growing apart.

4.

The Way Begins From Home

"El Camino de Santiago empieza en la puerta de la casa de cada uno.

The Way of Saint James starts at everyone's doorstep."
—Old Spanish Proverb

As a child my favorite day of the year was Christmas Eve. As far back as I can remember, our family spent it at 'Maw-maw' and 'Paw-paw's'—our dad's parents. Every December our family would load into our minivan and make the drive from where we were living in Texas (either Victoria or Beaumont) to their house in Gramercy, Louisiana. We would arrive on December twenty-second or twenty-third to settle in before the Christmas Eve Bonfire Festival—a nationally-visited spectacle of fires built along the levee of the Mississippi River.[vii] In late afternoon, aunts and uncles on our dad's side would arrive, joining a pre-bonfire celebration at Maw-maw and Paw-paw's where we would all eat jambalaya, labored away at by Uncle Stevie. We grandchildren would play together in Maw-maw and Paw-paw's backyard while adults sat at the dining room in the house talking. At six o'clock in the evening, our families would load into our cars and drive several miles to the levee alongside the Mississippi, where we would watch the bonfire lighting at seven o'clock in the evening. All of the children would light Black Cats and Roman Candles along the levee while adults drank beer in party tents alongside the River Road. After the fireworks were spent and the flames of the bonfires were waning, we would drive back to Maw-maw and Paw-paw's house and gather around Maw-maw to sing Christmas carols as she played the piano.

Our family never had lived nearby, so we would stay at Maw-maw and Paw-paw's house during Christmas time. This was one of the few times during the year where we would see Maw-maw, Paw-paw, our cousins, aunts and uncles. On New Year's Day, our family had the chance to say our good-byes until our family reunion in the summer. Then we would drive back to Texas.

This was always a bittersweet moment for me. While I always enjoyed the comfort of my own bed, I never liked the feeling of leaving behind Maw-maw and Paw-paw's house. They still lived in the Parish that my father's family had lived in for many generations. I missed being with our aunts, uncles and cousins. It always felt like we were the last to hear about new births or important events. Even as we drove home, I would long for the following Christmas and a return to Maw-maw and Paw-paw's.

In December of my junior year in high school, Maw-maw suffered a serious stroke. She lost movement on half her body, could no longer speak clearly, and became bedridden. Needless to say, we did not have a pre-bonfire

Christmas party at Maw-maw and Paw-paw's that year. Instead, all of her children and grandchildren took turns staying by her hospital bedside.

Just one month after Maw-maw's stroke—doctors met with our grandfather, my father and his five siblings to deliver grim news. She had suffered further strokes and was unlikely to recover. Faced with this news, our family made the decision to discontinue aggressive medical care, make her comfortable and bring her home. She died at home within several days, surrounded by her husband and six children.

My last memory of Maw-maw and Paw-paw's house was on their back porch at the picnic table after Maw-maw's funeral. Listening to the voices of my family from within the house, I was reminded of afternoons when Cory, our sister, our parents and I would sit and talk with Maw-maw as she labored away to cook crawfish etoufée. As sun began to set on the backyard, I noticed a few sparrows hopping from branch to branch on her oak tree, reminding me of the many mornings we would sit and watch birds eat from her bird feeder as she drank coffee.

As I relished the memories of Maw-maw evoked by sights and sounds from my perch at the picnic table, I realized that Maw-maw and Paw-paw's house had become for our family a *de facto* home. This was particularly true for Cory and me. Living in several different cities as children—Wilmington, North Carolina; Victoria, Texas; and Beaumont, Texas—Cory and I could never give a single answer when asked where we were from. We moved around at major junctures in our childhood—first when we were toddlers, then again when middle-schoolers—to cities that my dad's job brought us. We were much less rooted than our younger sister and our parents. Our sister Bethany spent most of her childhood in Victoria, Texas, and both our parents grew up and lived in the same area in Louisiana where they were born. Maw-maw and Paw-paw's house was, for Cory and me, a stable place we could count on returning to over the years.

In addition, in the short times that we visited Maw-maw and Paw-paw's, I felt as if Cory and I bonded much more than we did back in the hometown we were living in at the time. Not distracted by video or computer games, we spent more time visiting with each other. We played outside together more, either in their backyard or along nearby Blind River[viii]—neither of which we had access to in suburbia. And we spent more time helping out with dinner, eager to learn Maw-maw's Cajun recipes, which we both loved.

A year after Maw-maw's death, Paw-paw moved to an assisted living facility in Baton Rouge and their home Gramercy was sold. We would still go back to Gramercy for Christmas Eve celebrations, but with 'the old homestead' no longer a gathering place, I felt untethered. Before Maw-maw died, Gramercy always felt like home. After Maw-maw's funeral day, I did not return to Maw-maw and Paw-paw's. Without the anchor of their house, I struggled to answer the question of where home was.

***

Oviedo, Asturias, Spain

April 23, 2013

The sun shone brightly in the plaza in front of the Cathedral of Oviedo. Cory and I had to squint to make out the lone bell tower to the right of the main entrance. We were wide awake after a twelve-hour sleep at our hotel. After a breakfast of coffee, almond cake and nectar juice at the hotel bar, we took a walk to the Cathedral, going opposite the direction of the Way. The Cathedral would be our starting point, I told Cory.

The Cathedral of Oviedo was cast in a dim shadow as Cory and I entered. In the silence, we could hear our footsteps echo. At this earlier hour the tourist crowds had yet to arrive. Cory walked ahead of me as we strolled down the South end of the main transept towards the altar. His face bore an expression of equanimity, as if an earthquake could not alter his mood. Since he left prison, he seemed to have developed a tight regulation of his moods, making it difficult to distinguish from his facial expressions whether he was angry, apathetic or content.

As we neared the main altar, he stopped. In front of us lay the main altarpiece, the *retablo*—an ornate Flemish Gothic style multicolor carving.[ix] He coolly scanned the twenty-three scenes of the life of Christ as they traced two-thirds the way up the Cathedral dome. I stopped alongside him.

"Pretty overwhelming," I said, matter-of-factly.

He said nothing, as he continued to calmly scan the

altarpiece, which was not quite fully illuminated by the sunlight. After standing for a couple of minutes in front of the work, he walked slowly through the ambulatory behind the altar, on occasion stopping at a chapel to scan the layout, after which he would nod and move on to the next chapel.

I arrived at the ambulatory chapels after Cory. While I did not quite understand from his facial expressions how he felt about being there, I sensed from his wandering off that he was comfortable in experiencing the place on his own. We each continued, then, at our own paces. Once I had circled around to the other side of the altar, I come upon a well-lit side chapel.[x] Cory had continued on towards the Northern side of the main transept.

I stepped into the chapel and took a seat in a pew, placing my mochila beside me. I took a deep breath, closed my eyes, and tried to recall the sequence of events for the past thirty-six hours. From Houston we had flown to Newark. After a short the layover we flew on to Madrid. After landing, we spent the day walking around town before catching an evening flight to Oviedo. We checked into our hotel and went straight to sleep. After a good night's sleep, Cory and I had arrived at the start of our pilgrimage.

I opened my eyes. The morning sunlight from an east-facing window shone brightly on the dome above the altar, illuminating the elaborate gothic portico at the entrance to the chapel. A carving of the Virgin Mary, nursing the child Jesus, was positioned in the center of the doorway, dividing it in two. Flanking her on the outside of the doorway were stone carvings of the apostles Peter and Paul; further out to each side were James, on the left, and Andrew, on the right. I noted Saint James' pilgrim robe, daypack, and hat—emblazoned with a seashell on the front. I was struck with an uncanny feeling of providence as I took note of the parallel to my own jacket, backpack and alpine hat. The fact that Cory and I had made it here seemed no less miraculous than the miracle of thousands of pilgrims a millennia ago managing to weather the Asturian Mountains as they made their way to Santiago while the Moors occupied much of the Iberian Peninsula. No hindrances of our time—neither jail nor medical school nor financial struggles—had managed to prevent this trip.

Yet as I began to contemplate the upcoming pilgrimage, the uncertainties of my relationship with Cory filled my mind. There were so many unanswered questions that made me uncomfortable. Was Cory really as calm and even-tempered as he seemed? Or was he going to flip a switch and unleash his fury on me? Would he fall back into drugs on the trip? Would we even finish the pilgrimage?

As my peace turned to fear, I again closed my eyes. It was as if emerging from Plato's cave into the sun, fear drove me to retreat. I knew he had changed, but the past was impossible to forget. Trying to envision our future together, however, would be like looking at shadows on the wall in hopes of seeing reality more clearly. Clearly, what was behind me would be of no guidance for what lay ahead. I had no other choice but to turn to the present, letting our future unfold now, with whatever possibilities that lay ahead—even the possibility of being hurt.

As I opened my eyes, I noticed a confessional to the left of the chapel. In it was a Priest, peacefully perched reading a prayer book. Desperately hoping to talk to someone about Cory, I grabbed my *mochila,* walked over to the confessional, laid it beside me and knelt down.

Padre, necesito ayuda. I asked. ("Father, I need your help.")

The priest looked up from his prayer book and said:

Digame hijo. ("Tell me, son.")

***

Rice University, Houston, Texas
Fall 2007

During the fall of my senior year in college, I would visit with Father Justin, a friend who was chaplain of the Rice University Catholic Student Center. I connected with him through a mutual friend. Father Justin was a Benedictine monk from the UK. Prior to entering the priesthood, he had been a physician and psychological counselor. We met weekly for discussion, direction and just to develop our friendship.

During one of those discussions, I shared with him that

my parents were kicking Cory out of the house. After graduating from high school in Victoria, Cory had gone to Louisiana State University (LSU) for a couple of years, where he had continued drinking and using drugs. After having failed all of his classes—by fault of simply not showing up—my parents quit paying his tuition. He eventually ran out of money and returned to live with our parents in Victoria, Texas. There he continued with drugs and drinking, without any intention of getting back on his feet again to work. I recalled visiting home that previous summer, and when a friend of mine asked him what he was doing in life. He replied with a simple and fitting answer: "nothing." When my friend further queried him about what he planned to do, he was clear that his intention was to simply stay at home and not work. Once he'd made clear his lack of drive to find a job or re-enroll in school, my parents told him that he could no longer live with them any more.

Sitting in Father Justin's cozy office in the rectory, I shared my feelings of distress. I knew that Cory was suffering from addiction and was hurting himself. In that light, taking away the roof over his head seemed so drastic; forcing him out on the streets seemed so merciless. After I poured out my hurt, he looked at me and said:

"They are doing the right thing."

As I looked squarely at him, a tear swelled up in my eye. I refrained from blinking, hoping to keep it from running down my cheek. I did not want him to see me cry. If I knew he saw even a tear, he might take note, telling me it was okay to cry. I would be tempted to let loose all of my grief—which I was not prepared to do. The hurt was too deep to express.

"There comes a point when parents can't keep children from hurting themselves," he said. "If a grown child insists on self-destruction, then it may be the right decision to let him go…"

I sat silent for a moment, letting his words sink in. I held back my tears. To learn of my brother's struggles hurt so deeply, but I did not want to experience any more grief. The pain from the times when we were at home together was still too fresh. The scars had still not healed. The tear that had welled up ran down my face. Images of my brother roaming the streets without a home ran through my mind. I wanted to cry, but I was not ready.

Later that day, I let the tears come. I could not hold back the hurt that Cory's drug use caused me. I had hoped until then that I could just ignore his harmful habits. I would try to avoid every reminder of them. We had seen each other at Christmas and family vacations, but rarely in between. While we would exchange small talk at the dinner table or when we passed in the hallway, we would not discuss anything personal—not even what we were studying or whom we were dating. We'd almost never call each other. When my mom would tell me about his whereabouts, I would just listen and nod, daring not to ask too many questions. It's not that I had anything against him. Rather, I didn't want to experience the hurt of knowing that my own brother was hurting himself, and I couldn't do anything to stop it. I had hoped by avoiding reminders of his drug use, I could avoid the scars of the past, but I couldn't.

***

Cathedral of San Salvador, Oviedo, Asturias, Spain
April 23, 2013

I found Cory in front of the sculpture of Jesus at the South end of the transept, at the same point he stopped at to look at the altarpiece. He calmly scanned the image: a red and blue cloaked Iberian-looking Jesus holding a glass ball with the world in his left hand and holding up his three fingers in the sign of benediction with his right. I approached him from the side.

"Hi," I whispered.

"Oh, hi," he said, turning briefly to look at me. He turned back to looking at the image. I in turn stood next to him. As we stood in silence, admiring the historic sculpture, a few congregants began to enter a side-chapel. After a couple of minutes, the chapel began to fill and we heard entrance hymn to Mass emerging from it. Cory turned back to look at me.

"Did you want to go to Mass?" Cory asked.

I paused for a moment.

"No time," I replied. "We have to walk thirty kilometers

to get to the next *albergue*. If we don't leave now, we may get there too late."

At that he turned around and walked towards the exit through the main transept, the same way we entered. I followed.

As we neared the exit, I pulled out a devotion card from my pocket. The priest in the Chapel of the Chaste King had given it to me. I had expressed to him my worries about my future with Cory. He had listened intently as I told him that my brother was recently released from prison and that we were walking the Way to reconnect after a decade of separation. After expressing this to him, he looked at me calmly and—in Spanish—said:

"Sometimes life presents difficulties. That's why you are on this pilgrimage. Just as you carry the burden of your backpack each day, so too will you have burdens to carry with your relationship with your brother. But remember," he said, peering at me over his glasses, "every day is a new stage."

He then handed me a small devotional card.

"Do me a favor and say this prayer to Our Lady of Covadonga. Here in Asturias we have a special devotion to her."

I scanned over the card. On its front was a depiction of the traditionally venerated patroness of Asturias—a crowned young woman clad in royal red and white vestments.[xi] On its back was a prayer for her intercession in Asturian Spanish. I was puzzled at first by the gesture. It was hard to understand what this Iberian-looking depiction of the Virgin Mary had to do with my relationship with my recently incarcerated brother. Yet Father's words stuck with me.

"Every day is a new stage."

He used the word "*etapa*" for "stage," a word used in guidebooks to refer to discrete walks along the Way. Starting at one town and ending in another, each *etapa* would present its own route, architectural sites, places to sleep and diverse terrain. After soldiers petitioned the protection of Our Lady of Covadonga in battle against the Moors and successfully fought them off, pilgrims along the Primitive Way would petition her protection as they entered each new "etapa." Filled with dangers of inclement weather, thieves, disease and starvation, the Primitive Way came with no shortage of opportunities to petition her, and over the ages she became an icon of the Way's history.

As I pondered her importance, I realized that Father was not just inviting me to participate in a tradition that united pilgrims going back to the beginning of the Way. He was drawing me away from my worries about my future with my brother and asking me to focus on now—the pilgrimage ahead of me. I reached around to the side pocket in my backpack and grabbed my guidebook. Turning the page to the first *etapa*, I placed the devotional card in the book as a marker and returned the guidebook to its spot in my backpack.

We exited the Cathedral into the brightly lit plaza outside. For the first several kilometers, we walked through urban Oviedo, guided by bronze seashells cast into the sidewalk. Before leaving town, we stopped at a small supermarket, where Cory stocked up on anchovies, canned lentils and nuts. This would be his nourishment for the next couple of days, he said.

Eventually the urban sprawl thinned out, as the Way led us into smaller towns and eventually countryside. As we ascended in elevation, the beauty of the Asturian Mountains became apparent. The bright April sun shone on green hills that were occasionally interrupted with snow-capped peaks. A gentle breeze cooled as we walked the pastures in silence, save for the occasional cow moo.

With no more seashells cast into the sidewalk to guide us, yellow arrows painted on various objects along the way—guideposts, barns, and brick walls, guided us. These arrows, referred to as *flechas*, would keep us from wandering off track onto an abandoned field or a stray road. On occasion, instead of a *flecha*, we would come across a stone guidepost bearing a seashell, known on the Camino as a *concha*. The round end of the shell would point us in the direction of where to go.[xii] Whenever we would walk more than a half-mile without seeing a *concha* or a *flecha*, I would pull out my guidebook, nestled in the side pocket of my backpack, and check our place on the map. Every time I opened the book, I pulled out the devotion card to Our Lady of Covadonga, using it to mark the current *etapa*.

Jetlagged from the prior day's travels, we walked in relative silence for the first couple of hours. Groggy, I still felt asleep, even though I was awake and walking. Cory—though wide-awake—seemed as calm and even-tempered as he had in the Cathedral. It felt strange at first, to walk peacefully together. I wondered sometimes whether he would come up and bully push me—like he did in theater class. For the last ten years I had come to know him as jittery and on edge until then, but now he was meditative. As we continued our walk, sometimes stopping in chapels for a moment of silent meditation, I realized that Cory wasn't putting on a front. This really was him.

***

Houston, TX
December 2007

One evening in December of my senior year in college, I got an unexpected phone call from Cory. I was sitting at my desk in my apartment in Houston when he called my cell phone.

"Cory?" I said, surprised that he would call. He never called me when he was not in a sober period, which I didn't think he was. As my mom told me, he did indeed leave home in the Fall. He had gone to live with our maternal grandmother, Meime. She lived in West Greensboro, North Carolina and was willing to take him in, even if he was struggling with addiction.

"Brother, I have to tell you something," he proclaimed.

My heart started racing. There was an urgency in his voice. Worst-case scenarios came to mind. Had he been abducted? Was he hospitalized? Was he in jail?

"What's up?" I asked, quizzically.

"I've been doing some reading here with Meime, and the stuff she showed me is pretty convincing. The world's going to end in six to nine months. I'm sure of it."

"What?" I exclaimed. "Are you high? Have you been drinking?"

I could not believe the words coming out of his mouth. He sounded sober and serious.

"No, I'm serious. I've quit doing drugs and drinking since getting here. Meime's convinced me of this. I'm absolutely certain it's going to happen," he went on.

"What makes you think that?" I asked, still incredulous.

"Meime's been showing me some ancient prophecies that predicted exactly the current events that we're seeing now. Those same prophecies predict that the world's going to end six to nine months later. I just want to make sure you're okay before the world ends."

I rolled my eyes. Meime had recently joined a group that adopted Jewish customs, who believed in the imminent coming of a Messiah. They were not Jews, but would eat Kosher food and celebrate Jewish holidays. This was not her first time to try to scare our family with Chicken

Little scenarios. When I was a child, she was always worried about doomsday scenarios. First, the world was going to end in the year 2000 when computer crashes were predicted to cause social mayhem. Then, when that didn't happen, 9/11 was supposed to be the beginning of some galactic battle that ended the human race. Then when that didn't happen, the year 2012—the end of the Mayan calendar—was supposed to be the next supposed end. She had no dearth of doomsday theories.

Hearing this, I was upset. She caught him at a vulnerable time. He was homeless and addicted. But this was not what he needed. This would not last for long with him. He was too smart, I knew, to be pulled into this. He would not likely believe this for another month, much less the 6 to 9 months it would take to for him to see that his prediction wouldn't happen.

For the next half hour, I tried to convince him against falling into the trap of believing all-encompassing scare theories. I brought up the many-failed historical doomsday movements, going back to the fall of Rome. He wasn't swayed. Then I reminded him of Meime's recurring end of the world theories that never came to pass. He still wasn't moved. "This one is real," he said.

We finally just had to end the conversation as cordially as possible. We agreed to disagree.

"I hope you'll realize that the world's going to end," were his parting words.

I hung up the phone, tense.

Cory and I had not engaged in a serious argument since high school. After the scuffle in the laundry room, I avoided any confrontation with him. Arguments brought up fears of physical confrontation, or worse, rejection. It was easier to stay free and clear of the minefield that I had not mapped.

This time, however, I felt uneasy for different reasons. I could sense from the urgency in his voice that he genuinely thought he was helping me, yet his reasoning felt like it came out of nowhere. That is what made me uneasy. It seemed bizarre—not typical of Cory. Ever since rehab, he had renounced organized religion, insisting that any single religion was too narrow to encompass the wealth of human paths to reach the divine. Such a quick acceptance of (what I considered) extreme beliefs made me worried that something more sinister lay behind his new-found obsession.

I sat at my desk, phone in hand and looked out the window. Night had begun to fall. I thought of what I would do if I were without a home at night. I would probably call someone close to me as he did with Meime. Yet I would still be shocked. Then it occurred to me: Cory was in shock. He had just been kicked out of our parents' house. Shock explained his embrace of such dramatic beliefs. While homeless, Meime offered him a home, and in a state of shock, he might believe her proselytizing. In this state of shock over being homeless, he was soaking up her end of the world fears. His addiction had led him to rock bottom, and he was searching for meaning—meaning to pull him out of the meaninglessness of addiction.

How long, I wondered, would it be until he came to his senses? This state would not last for long. He would either find a new set of beliefs or go back to drugs and alcohol. I just hoped he was not let too far astray in the meantime.

***

Somewhere outside Oviedo, Asturias
April 23, 2013

Around mid-afternoon Cory and I came upon a small church on the Way. Nestled on the side of the road, its front was adorned with several types of quarried stone. I gestured to enter.

"I'm going to stop at this chapel. Do you want to come?" I said to Cory, walking not more than twenty feet ahead. He had stopped briefly to admire the exterior, but after a half-minute, he kept walking.

"Okay," he said, following me as I entered the door. Inside, the chapel was empty. Its interior was dark, granting us shade from the warm, afternoon sun. With no traffic on the road, the place was silent. I took off my hat and backpack, lying them down in a back pew, and sat down. Cory sat down next to me, still holding his backpack with one arm. We sat in silence, admiring the simplicity of this rural church.

After a couple of minutes, Cory leaned over and whispered: "Any idea where the other pilgrims are?"

Up until that point, we hadn't met any pilgrims. Compared to the throngs of pilgrims Amanda and I came across on the French Way, this was indeed a change.

"Not sure," I whispered. "This is surprising me too."

"I guess it's just me and you," I continued.

We grabbed our *mochilas*, exited and kept walking.

By then it was morning in Texas, so I grabbed my phone to check if Amanda had called.
She hadn't.

"Do you have signal?" Cory asked.

"Not here," I said. "It's hit or miss in these mountains."

"Are you using mom and dad's plan?" he asked.

"No," I said. "I got a phone card from Orange while we were in Plaza del Sol."

"Oh," he said. "I guess I was too busy watching the protestors to notice."

He was referring to the *indignados*—a group of protestors in Madrid, angered by the grave economic situation in

Spain. We had come across some of them in the Plaza del Sol in Madrid.

As we continued to walk, we talked about the protests that were taking place. He asked what I knew of the reasons they were protesting. I told him that from what I knew of the Spanish economy, jobs for youth were sparse, leading to mass protests such as the one we witnessed. He chuckled and then said they should go to Mexico to get jobs. I laughed.

He then told me about a Mexican drug-lord who he shared a prison cell with in the MCC. As a wealthy drug dealer, he said, this guy was well versed in how to run a business. Cory recounted how the drug-lord was knowledgeable of economic opportunities in Mexico. The country was a fertile place to start a small business, Cory went on.

I then interjected: "Aren't some areas in Mexico dangerous though?"

He didn't respond to my question and continued talking about small businesses as the answer to economic decline. Eventually, I told him about my plans to start a medical practice. He seemed interested in my business plan. We continued talking about small business planning, so immersed in conversation that we nearly missed the turn for the *albergue*.

We came on a diversion for the *albergue* of San Juan de Villapañada some two kilometers (about a mile) outside of Grado, the largest town we had passed since Oviedo.

Walking there, I wondered whether we were even going to find anyone when we got there. Still, we hadn't yet seen any other pilgrims. When we arrived, however, several were seated at a picnic table in front; the first pilgrims we had seen all day. Their faces looked uneasy when we approached. Maybe it was my alpine hat that tipped them off to the fact that we were foreigners.

"Bienvenidos," said a tall, broad-shouldered soldier-looking man with a crew cut.

"Do you want to sit down?" he said, in Spanish, moving over to make enough space for one of us to squeeze in. Another professor-looking pilgrim with scruffy hair and dark-rimmed glasses got up and gestured for one of us to sit.

"I don't want to take anyone's seat," I said, in my not-quite-native sounding Spanish.

"Don't worry, I need to stretch my legs," said the professor.

Cory and I laid our backpacks down on the ground and sat at the table. I introduced us as brothers from Texas—one from Houston and the other from Austin. They were all Spanish. The soldier was Omar, an aspiring police officer from Andalucía. The professor was Juan, a recent law graduate from the Sorbonne in Paris who was originally from Murcia. With them sat Alfonso, a skinny older man from the Islas Baleares. Standing at the head of the table was Domingo, the *hospitalero*, who had his hands sprawled out on Omar's map of the Primitive

Way. He had been pointing out worthy places to eat and sleep along the Way.

We all small talked. Cory followed along as we spoke in Spanish. As long as the comments were short, he could understand and give one-sentence replies. (His Spanish had remarkably improved in the MCC San Diego.) After chatting for a few minutes, Domingo, the *hospitalero* standing at the head of the table, invited Cory and me to settle into the *albergue*.

We entered the cabin, found the sleeping area, a small room no larger than twenty feet by twenty feet lined with bunk beds—and each laid our backpacks on a bed. Laying a backpack on a bed is a universal sign to other pilgrims the bed is occupied. (To remove a bag from a bed would be an unspoken violation of pilgrim ethics.) After taking out our pillows and unrolling our sleeping bags, we each showered and then divvied up chores. I would do the laundry, for which there was—thankfully—a washing machine. Cory would cook dinner. After gathering our sweaty clothes and making rounds to gather garments from other pilgrims, I started a load of laundry. Meanwhile Cory chopped calamari and vegetables, a job for which he enlisted the help of Juan and Omar, both of whom would join us for dinner.

With a few minutes to spare before dinner, I slipped away to take a small walk. A few minutes away lay a five hundred year-old Church built by the Knights of the Order of Malta I wanted to visit.[xiii] The Church's front doors, however, were locked. I walked around in the courtyard, hoping that maybe there was another entrance.

I couldn't find one. Disappointed, I walked back to the *albergue.*

As I neared the *albergue*'s front door, I could hear the voices of Cory, Juan and Omar from outside as they chopped vegetables in preparation for Cory's squid pasta. I paused. The sound of their voices conjured a feeling of *déjà vu.* I felt as if I had once been there, though I had never been on the Primitive Way. I was perturbed.

Sitting at the picnic table in front of the albergue, I jogged my memory. I tried to recall when in the past I might have been there. I could not remember, though. After a few minutes, my mind wandered. I turned my attention to the sparrows hopping from branch to branch in a nearby tree.

As I got up to go inside for dinner, I remembered. It was Maw-maw and Paw-paw's. My memory was playing tricks on me, substituting memory of a feeling for memory of a place. I recalled having an open, honest conversation with my brother—uninhibited by distraction of drugs or fears of retaliation—on a visit to Maw-maw and Paw-paw's. We had spent the day canoeing and swimming on Blind River and we were welcomed to Maw-maw's kitchen for a home-cooked meal of crawfish etoufée. Now, in San Juan de Villapañada, some ten years later, we had spent the day hiking the Asturian Mountains. We had moreover bonded talking about small-business planning. At the end of the day, we had come to a home-cooked meal, this time made by Cory in the *albergue* kitchen. We were thousands of miles from Louisiana, and yet I felt as if we were back at home—even if only for a night.

5.
A New 'Etapa'

Cada kilómetro recorrido en el Camino, cada etapa, es como un momento de tu vida, duro y largo, pero con recompensas

Every kilometer on the road, each step is like a moment of your life, hard and long, but with rewards
–Pilgrim on the Way of Saint James

San Juan de Villapañada, Asturias
April 24, 2013

The sun shone brightly as we began walking on the Way. Cory and I began our hike through low-lying green hills under completely cloudless blue skies. Dew, condensed on the ripe pastures, wet our shoes as we walked, dampening our socks. We were the last ones out of the albergue, but I wasn't bothered. We were awake and full of energy, fueled by a full night's sleep. The day was fresh and promising as we began our climb in elevation to the peak of Fresno. The weather was ideal; the terrain, a balanced mix of elevations and descents, giving our leg muscles a formidable but not unsurpassable challenge.

Juan walked with us that morning. He, like us, was also a late sleeper. In between occasional remarks about the scenery, he began to tell us what led him to walk the Primitive Way. He embarked on the Way after graduating from the University of Sorbonne with a law degree. Limited by a competitive job market, he walked the Way in search of guidance over where to go next in his career. He had been told, moreover, of the growing crowds on the French Way and sought a more tranquil path to Santiago de Compostela. He had departed from Oviedo the day before, as we had. Somehow we missed crossing paths.

After walking for about an hour, we came upon a small village called Doriga. At the entrance of the town was a mom-and-pop looking bar.[xiv] Juan and I agreed to enter. Cory, however, decided he would keep walking.

"I'm not hungry," he said. Earlier, he had eaten leftovers from the dinner he cooked for pilgrims the night before: pasta with vegetables and squid. I was not hungry but did not want to miss the chance for coffee when bars were so few and far between.

We agreed to meet ahead. If he got to Cornellana, the next town, he would stop and wait for us. At that, he kept walking, while Juan and I entered the bar.

Inside we met Antonio, the bartender. Groggy-eyed and slow to move, he welcomed us as friends who had just stumbled in. He began talking about the soccer match the night before. Valencia and Osasuna had gone into overtime.

"Did you see it?" he asked us.

Neither of us had. After telling us how exciting the game was –so much so that he was up late watching it –he solicited for our order.

We each ordered a coffee. He then slipped away, informing us before he left that it would take several minutes to percolate. As I sat at the bar with Juan, I noted on the far end of the bar a black-and-white portrait hung on the wall. When he returned with our coffee, he saw me admiring the photo. "My grandparents," he said in his thick Asturian Spanish. The woman was Maria Abello de la Paz, "la Pacita," a Cuban woman who nearly single handedly built up the business into an icon for the town. He had come, only a few years ago, to take over the business. The move served him well, he said. The business had grown alongside the increased pilgrim traffic on the Primitive Way.

After a fresh cup of coffee, Juan and I left to catch up with Cory. Cory had advanced too far ahead, however, to catch up in the next village. Eventually, Juan asked why Cory and I had decided to walk the Way together.

I paused for a moment.

Not knowing how to answer the question, I said:

"Bueno…" (Spanish for "well…") just letting the word trail off as I tried to grasp for words. I was conflicted. Trying to think of an answer, I vacillated in my mind for a minute—going back and forth between not answering and letting out a whole childhood history. I wanted to be candid, but I feared that words alone could not express why Cory and I embarked on the Primitive Way. The wrong description of Cory's past could lead to undue stigma. Eventually, I answered.

"My brother was imprisoned for several years. We didn't have chance to see each other during that time. He was just released in February. This is our chance to reconnect."

"Wow," he said, scrunching his eyebrows in surprise. He kept walking in silence, letting the news sink in. Then, without a pretense of judgment, asked:

"In the US, prisons are quite harsh aren't they?"

"Well, he was in a federal prison, which is not as bad as some state prisons, but yes, in general, life is quite harsh in our prisons."

"That's rough," he said. He seemed more surprised than bothered. It was as if I had just told him that our mother had died or that we had come together after being separated at birth. It was sad news, but he cast no condemnation.

After a few minutes, the subject of my brother was forgotten, and we began to talk about the job market for young lawyers in Europe. This led to a discussion on labor markets for young workers in the continent, a topic that then opened up the broad topic of Europe's economy. We could not avoid the topic. We were two young professionals at the beginning of our careers. For over an hour, we explored the topic in detail, lamenting the unsightly paradoxes of capitalism and socialism, as we had both witnessed them play out in our respective countries.

We came across Cory waiting for us at the other side of the bridge over the Narcea River—just outside the entrance to Cornellana.

"Were you waiting for us the entire time?" Juan asked.

"Yeah."

"What did you do?" he asked.

"Well, I was thinking of wading in the river for a while," Cory replied, looking down at the river.

"Are you crazy? That's dangerous! The water is dirty." Juan chided.

"No, I just wanted to wet my feet,"

He grabbed his backpack and followed us as we walked into town. After crossing the River Narcea, Cory, Juan and I entered the town of Cornellana through its main road, Avenue Prudencio Fernandez Pe. Known for its thousand year-old monastery, Cornellana struck me as a living exhibit of European history, nestled in the Asturian Mountains.[xv] The city's old town clustered around the ruins of the monastery, since abandoned, while the more recent development—by 'recent' I mean the last century—clustered around Avenue Prudencio Fernandez Pe. Along this thoroughfare lay storefronts and homes all comprised of a patchwork of clay, stucco, brick and natural stone—some of which surely came from the monastery after its seizure and partial dismantling by Napoleonic troops.

We all decided to stop for coffee break after entering town. Juan sat at a table in front of a street side coffee shop—one of the two in town. We followed suit. Within minutes we were drinking espressos and eating "*carajitos*"—a rich almond cookie especially made in Cornellana. Short for "Carajitos del Profesor," carajitos take their name from Professor Falon, a music director (often called "Professor") from the nearby town of Salas who owned a bar in the early 1900's and whose son would bake hazelnut cookies for clients to have with their afternoon coffee. The name came from a certain South American gentleman, who had the audacity to order a "*carajo*" (perhaps best translated as a "shit-load") of these cookies.

As Cory and I sat sipping our espressos and eating *carajitos*, Juan went inside. He came back out with a newspaper and laid it on the table, perusing the headlines. The front page bore a photo of protestors in Madrid.

"The situation is very bad," he said, in Spanish, throwing the newspaper down on the table.

"Why do you think about the protestors?" I inquired.

"The *indignados* have it all wrong," he said. "They don't have a mission. They just want to protest and not provide an alternative."

"What are they even protesting?" Cory asked, derisively.

"Plenty of corruption," Juan said.

"Seems like they could be doing something constructive with that energy. If the system is broken, whey don't they rebuild instead of destroy it?" Cory asked.

"Good question," Juan answered as he stared into the road. After a few seconds he shook his head and looked back at Cory.

"So, Cory, what are you going to do?" Juan asked.

"Not sure. I'm thinking of buying some investments...maybe real estate or stocks that I could live on...just enough to supply the minimum amount of income that I need to live on. Then with the rest of my time I could spend it volunteering for worthy causes to better the community…urban gardening, helping out strangers, or just random acts of kindness."

"Wow, sounds cool," he said. "Good luck."

As we were finishing our coffees, the bartender came outside to chat. He was surprised at the weather.

"This is the best weather we've had in a while," he said. "Around here it's two good days then three bad ones."

We laughed in disbelief.

He also told us that many pilgrims—perhaps a dozen—had come by en route to Bodenaya. They were headed to Alejandro's *albergue*—the one we were told not to miss by Domingo. We were the day's stragglers. After a brief chat with him we grabbed our backpacks and continued on our Way.

We arrived at Salas, the next major town, by early afternoon—around two o'clock. Along the main street we found a restaurant with a seashell posted next to the door. (A seashell icon posted outside of a restaurant or hotel was a sign that pilgrims were given special attention.) Casa Pachón[xvi]—the place was called. This was the place recommended by Domingo, I recalled. "There you'll eat really well," he said.

As soon as we entered the cozy diner, the owner, a scruffy energetic redhead, immediately welcomed us. Rough, rowdy and informal but clearly warm-hearted, he reminded me of a Spanish version of my Uncle Clifford. "Here, you're going to eat well," he tells us, as he pulls out chairs for us and sets our places at the table. Cory, Juan and I sat together in the back. The redhead scurried off for several minutes before returning.

"What are you going to eat? The *menú* ?" he asked. The *menú* was referred a fixed price menu, common on the Camino and usually consisting of a first course (soup or salad), second course (a meat) and dessert.

"Yes, I'll get the *menú*," Juan said. The redhead looked at me, expectantly.

"The same," I said.

"The *menú* is very good," he said. "You will like it. If you're still hungry at the end, we'll give you more," he said.

"And you," he said, looking at Cory. "What are you going to eat?"

"Is it possible," Cory said, "just to try some soup?"

"Of course," he said. "Do you want me to get you a bowl?"

Cory hesitated. "Uh, sure."

After a few minutes, the redhead came out with the first course: lentil soup. Cory ate half the bowl and then stopped eating.

"I'm full. I'm going to keep walking. Can I pay you back for the soup?"

"Don't worry about it," I said.

He grabbed his *mochila* and departed, agreeing to meet me in Bodenaya.

Juan and I stayed to consume the rest of the pilgrim's menu—a six course array of lentil soup, vegetable soup, Cuban rice, fish over fries and our choice of custard, rice pudding or fruit for dessert.

Satiated, I walked at a slow pace to Bodenaya. Juan passed me quickly after we left Casa Pachón, and for the rest of the afternoon, I walked alone. The bright Asturian sun above me, I could not have asked for a more picturesque walk. Cory had walked much further, but I didn't mind that. He was going at his own pace. He, like me, needed his solitude at times. I wanted Cory to feel as much in control of this trip as I was—it was our trip after all. We would meet again in Bodenaya.

After walking for an hour, my phone rang. It was Amanda. She was calling from Houston, where she was back teaching. It was her off period. Benny, she said, was nursing voraciously. She began to tell me how glad she was that Cory and I could go on this pilgrimage together. After about a minute, we were cut off. The mountains were too far off for 3G to have coverage. We would have to pick up the conversation later.

***

Houston, TX

June 27, 2009

After our argument over the end of the world, Cory and I didn't talk for a while. The end of the world did not come, and regrettably, Cory had started drinking again. I didn't speak to him again until a year later. For the weekend of my wedding, he came to the rehearsal dinner the day before, but we did not have time to talk amidst the excitement of family members arriving out of town. On the morning of the wedding, prior to the ceremony, we met in the entrance lobby of the Cathedral at the entrance to the doors. He graciously agreed to be an usher along with Amanda's older brother. Thin, well-tanned and bearing a tux, he looked nothing like what I had imagined a year ago when he was homeless and seeking refuge in the mountains of Appalachia.

There were a few minutes before the ceremony would start and guests had yet to arrive, giving us a little time to talk.

"Thanks for the surprise you left me," I said, wryly. Cory along with my best man, Mark, and two other friends, had completely rearranged the furniture in the wedding suite in my hotel room. He snorted with laughter.

"Just keeping you on your toes."

After a few seconds of silence, he said, "Amanda told me you guys were in Austin on 6th street a few weeks ago. Why didn't you come see me? I live right there."

Amanda and I had been in Austin three weeks earlier for the wedding of my best man Mark. I did not contact Cory in part because we did not have much time. But more than that, I wasn't comfortable with calling him. I didn't know whether he was still drinking or on drugs. I did not want to risk another argument. It was easier to play it safe and avoid him.

"We had a busy weekend," I sheepishly responded.

"Well, I'm really happy for you two," he said, changing

the subject. He had glow in his eyes that I had not seen before.

***

Bodenaya, Asturias
April 24, 2013

When I arrived at Bodenaya Alejandro—the *hospitalero*—was waiting in front of the *albergue* to greet new pilgrims. A young, tall quiet gentleman, he showed me where to place my shoes alongside a rack in a polar entry-type room before entering the main *albergue*. I asked him if my brother had arrived already.

"Ah yes, the American kid, he's upstairs." He showed me into the main room of the *albergue*—a cozy single room with hardwood floors and a small kitchen with a minibar and wooden barstools situated at the far end of the entry doors. On the left was a wooden picnic table, seated next to a stone-wall. On the opposite end of the room from the table was a narrow, wooden stairwell, which led to two small rooms filled with bunk beds.

I found Cory in the far room, where he had claimed one of the bottom beds. We greeted each other and embraced. He had reserved the top bunk for me. I thanked him and placed my backpack on the bunk. As I began to unpack, a young, slender Asian woman entered. She introduced herself and placed her massive backpack on the adjacent bunk bed. She was from South Korea, she said, and was in Spain on vacation. Not knowing how much to pack, she told us, she packed everything she thought of. In the end, her backpack weighed 40 pounds--probably more than a third of her body weight. Cory continued to talk to her while I unpacked and went downstairs to shower.

After showering, I went to the main room downstairs. Alejandro was busy chopping vegetables. I offered to help, but he had several helping hands and declined assistance. Cory was there sitting at the table along with several other pilgrims. Noticing a crowded dining table with no empty space to sit, I sat at a smaller table near the staircase. Looking around, I noticed a photo album on a bookshelf just next to the table. I pulled out the album, placed it on the table and opened it. In it were photos of the albergue before it was restored. The house was in ruins; the grain silo, falling apart. This was in 2006 Alejandro, then a taxi driver in Madrid, sold his taxi and medallion, bought the house and restored it. He had been inspired after walking the Primitive Way himself. As I flipped the pages, further photos chronicled a year of hard work restoring the house, he had created this gem of hospitality for pilgrims along the Primitive Way. This was his full time job now.

As I flipped through the album, Cory interrupted me. He invited me to play chess with him.

"Well, I haven't played it in a while," I said. I did not really want to play. I never much enjoyed the game.

"Just once. Come on."

I agreed to play.

He set down the chess board next to me and sat at the seat across. I set down the album and moved the pawn forward. We continued making moves on the chessboard as we talked about the day's walk. He had beat me in less than twenty moves.

"Nobody could beat me in prison," he chortled.

***

New York, New York
October *15, 2009*

After the wedding, I didn't hear from Cory again for several months later. By then, Amanda and I were living in New York City, and Cory had returned to Austin. He wrote me a touching email.

Things are pretty good over here... It's warm and sunny outside after a week of cold cloudy misty weather. The monarchs are fluttering through town on their way to Mexico... I'm taking the day off. My boss stayed up too late and didn't make it to work in time to let me know to stay. So I thought I'd get some things accomplished and call/email people I have been wondering about.. You were at the top of my list...

It's a peculiar place to be, here almost 8 years since I've put any good faith into the power of the greater good. It's truly amazing to me how from where we are standing now things behind and before us can be so well hidden. I feel this way about my spiritual journey. Looking back it's tempting to be regretful or wonder how I could be so close to life and disregard it in favor of indulgence or any lesser path for that matter. But in reality I have never been able to look forward and see the way out without simply climbing one rock higher…

He described how living in Austin helped him "climb one rock higher." He was still doing construction and landscaping work, as he had been doing in North Carolina, but he was making time to contribute to projects he saw meaningful in the community. He was cooking breakfast every Sunday for a community of ecstatic dancers—a group of freestyle dancers who would shake it to any type of music, ranging from African jungle rhythm to Michael Jackson, in a group setting. He was also volunteering for upkeep of Barton Springs—an ancient spring now converted into a swimming area outside of Austin. Sometimes, he would just take a day to reconnect with a childhood friend he hadn't seen before.

He made a point, moreover, that his community service would never be compromised by his need to make a living. This usually meant living day to day, but he preferred the freedom to pursue fulfillment of immaterial needs to the security of material ones.

It seemed clear that he was winning his battle with addiction. I was touched that he reached out to write me. Though he seemed calm and cool at the wedding, I still was unsure of whether he wanted a relationship with me. Eager to reconnect with him, I replied with a lengthy email expressing my joy for him finding a renewed sense of purpose. I encouraged him to continue his community service and seeking ways that he could contribute to the greater good. I also proposed that we plan a trip together during my next vacation from medical school, making a chance to reconnect after so many years adrift. He replied: "I wouldn't miss it. Talk soon, Cory."

***

Bodenaya, Asturias
April 25, 2013

After being soundly defeated by Cory in chess, I wandered upstairs, in search of my guidebook and journal. Prior to journaling about the day's events, I planned to review the next day's itinerary – sites that lie ahead, what not to miss, where to eat, and where to sleep.

I pulled out the guidebook from the side pocket of my backpack and sat on the bottom bunk to read it, opening the guidebook to the next *etapa*: Salas to Tineo—19 kilometers (12 miles). Bodenaya, a small accumulation of houses along the road, was some two kilometers (one mile) beyond Salas. The next day's goal would be to walk to Tineo: 17 kilometers (11 miles). As I flipped through to the next page, I pulled out the place marker I had used to mark the etapa we were walking: the devotional card bearing Our Lady of Covadonga. Father's words came to mind. "Every day is a new etapa."

The words were fitting for Cory and me. We had entered a new stage with each other. Our past was still there, but it was behind us. He was no longer succumbing to his addictions. While still quirky, I saw in him a genuine change—for the better. As I looked at the devotional card, voices from the kitchen called up. It was dinner time. I placed the devotional card back into my guidebook and lay it on my bed.

Downstairs, Alejandro—with the assistance of other pilgrims--prepared a hearty dinner of salad, lentil stew and bread. I ate little, still satiated from my meal at Casa Pachón. After dinner, all pilgrims retired upstairs to sleep. Exhausted from another long walk, I fell asleep quickly. I was awoken the next morning to the gentle Gregorian chanting of *Ave Maria* Alejandro turned on to lure us out of bed. I slowly rustled around in bed before climbing down from the top bunk and heading downstairs for the light breakfast Alejandro had prepared. Cory had already gone down. It was time to begin a new *etapa*.

6.
And Then Came The Rain

"Que el camino salga a tu encuentro. Que el viento siempre esté detrás de ti y la lluvia caiga suave sobre tus campos.

May the Way meet you where you are. May the wind always be behind you and the rain fall soft upon your fields."
—Celtic prayer

El Pedregal, Asturias
April 25, 2013

Dirty rain-water sloshed into my shoes with each step on the earthen road outside El Pedregal. Even the slightest splash aggravated the blisters on my feet. Drops soaked my poncho, converged and dripped onto the mush below. After two days of sunshine, the clouds came. The saying by the people of the Asturian Mountains proved true: "two good days then three bad ones." The soft, gentle *Ave Maria* that lured us out of bed in Bodenaya hailed the end of our honey-moon with the Primitive Way. As soon as we departed the albergue, rain started falling. Rain then mixed with snow, and the country road turned into asphalted highway for the first half of the walk.

Cory ran ahead of me not long after the rain began. Initially, he walked within sight, but after half an hour, he had too much energy for me to keep up. He said that he had to sprint periodically to use up his energy. The sight was strange, seeing a young pilgrim along the highway doing sprints like a football player, but knowing that this was Cory, the same person who would run barefoot around Austin for miles, I was unsurprised. So as we did the day before, Cory and I walked apart for much of the morning.

Juan, who departed Bodenaya when we did, walked at my pace as Cory ran ahead. When Juan saw Cory sprinting, he looked surprised.

"What's your brother doing?" he asked.

"He's going at his own rhythm," I replied, shaking my head. I laughed.

Juan looked perplexed. I didn't care to explain, nor could I. He was not in a hurry, I was certain, but why he sprinted ahead was a question whose answer I could not articulate.

For much of the morning Juan and I continued our discussion of Europe's economy, a topic that by then we had discussed *ad nauseum*. Juan bemoaned fiscal imbalances in Spanish regional government's budgets; I, the U.S. Gross National Debt. As our commentary took a cynical turn, Juan in his wisdom abruptly but politely asked that we change subjects, after which point we continued in silence for a short time. Juan eventually outpaced me as we veered off the highway near El Pedregal.

Alone, I trekked on as the icy rain pounded against my poncho. It would occasionally lighten, only to return with a new fury. Thick, cumulonimbus rain-clouds poured out unrelenting droplets onto my poncho. Dripping down from my shoulders, they drenched the uncovered wrist-portion of nylon jacket. I was discouraged.

It was not the wetness itself that bothered me. Coming from Texas, I was used to sweat. Rather, the cold, damp moisture on my forearms reminded me that I could have warm and dry forearms were I at home in Houston. The slosh that seeped into my shoes, which by then I had learned were certainly not waterproof or even water resistant, caused my toes to tingle at their tips, leading me to question why I left behind Amanda, Benny and our cozy, warm condominium in Houston. Why was I not lying down, dry in our queen-size bed holding Benny? Why was I not reading *Lord of the Rings*, lying back on our living room loveseat?

I continued in silence along dirt roads and muddy streams from El Pedregal to the neighborhood of San Roque, just outside Tineo, until I came upon a cast iron statue of a pilgrim perched ten feet off the Way to the left. The stick-figure statue stood tall holding his cape with his left hand and in his right a walking stick with a squash gourd on the top. His cape bore a *concha* in the middle. He stood on a seashell marked in straight lines with each ray of the shell marked by a Roman numeral I-XII. Beneath the shell and inscription in Latin read—

Viator Horam Aspice et Abi Viam Tuam. "Traveler, look at the time and continue your way."[xvii]

Onward, I continued to walk.

After a one-hundred meter descent from San Roque to Tineo, I passed through the Avenue Gonzales Mayo in Tineo to the central plaza, where Cory was nowhere to be found. I knew that he had at least made it to San Roque because a couple of teenage boys resting in a park Gazebo alongside the Way told me that they saw a pilgrim jogging down the hill. No pilgrim other than Cory would jog. Still, I could not find him, despite pacing up and down Gonzales Mayo Avenue—from town entrance to City Hall. Fortunately, rain had subsided by then, though skies were still overcast. I must have made the same back-and-forth round-trip three or four times. After nearly an hour of pacing back and forth through Tineo, I did get word from a bar-tender that he had "just passed by" not more than an hour ago, yet our paths never seemed to cross. I even went past the turnoff for the Way to the outskirts of town, passing the police station, a sight that for a moment made my pulse accelerate.

Worst-case scenarios would come to mind when Cory was missing. *What if he slipped and injured himself? What if he couldn't find his way in the rain and took a nose-dive off a cliff? What if he simply wandered off the way and ends up in another city?* ...silly questions which—though neurotic—I had to acknowledge as arising from a primordial sense of protectiveness. Familial protectiveness—though healthy—has its way of turning into fear. This particularly true with Cory. Ever since he went to drug rehab, I feared for his wellbeing. Even when he was clean and sober, I feared that he would suffer from relapse and make a decision in his addiction that would be fatal. Judy's exhortation to Cory came to mind: "you only have three places to go: jail, institutions or death. You are already in an institution. I know you have legal problems. Where else is there for you to go?"

***

New York, New York
July 2010

It was on a muggy New York afternoon that I found out about my brother's accident. After arriving at our Upper East Side studio apartment, my clothes already wet from the seven block walk home from the hospital, I sat down at our kitchen table. Then my wife casually informed me while cooking dinner that "you know your brother had an accident right?" Having not heard any news regarding Cory, I didn't even register what she meant. *Did he pee his pants or did a car hit him?* I wondered. On asking her for clarification it was to my total surprise the latter—hit by a car—a response which nearly gave me a heart attack until she informed me, still calmly as can be, that "it happened about a month ago. He got pretty banged up but he's okay." My jaw dropped as I sat at our kitchen table, totally aghast that I had not yet heard of this until she followed up the news with advice to "look at the email your mom sent you about it."

Sure enough, in my inbox, my mom had sent me an

email on June 9—over one month prior to me finding out—with the subject "Cory was hit by a car." In it, she explained that while on an evening bike ride with a group of friends, Cory—who, riding straight on a green light, had the right of way—kept riding through the intersection. The driver, however, turned left on an unprotected green light while he rode full speed in the opposite direction. The car hit Cory with full impact. While he did lose consciousness, she noted, he did not suffer any broken bones or internal bleeding seen on imaging. He was simply treated in the emergency room for a facial laceration and discharged the same day. In the process, he lost his wallet and phone and incurred a $25,000 emergency room bill, for which he had neither the health insurance nor the money to pay.

Reading my mom's email was reassuring in some senses to know that he had he had not suffered any critical injury—nor lost his life for that matter—but it was also an eye-opening reminder of how, after starting medical school, my family and I had not been able to maintain as regular contact as before. Nearly two years passed since I visited my parents' home. While we would normally talk on the phone weekly, there was no substitute for their physical presence nearby. I had, however, sacrificed nearness to my family in exchange for an Ivy League education. On reading her email, I began to question whether the sacrifice was worth it. Should I have stayed in Texas for medical school? Why didn't I just stay home and become a high school teacher?

***

Tineo

April 25, 2013

I found Cory at a bar on Avenida Gonzales Mayo. Before he saw me, I caught a glimpse of his face. I could see the white of his eyes—not quite tearful but still and sullen, like a child lost in a department store. His eyebrows crinkled. His worry was apparent. Usually fearless in the face of danger, he caught me off guard.

"Where were you?" I asked, somewhat exasperated.

"I tried looking for you but when I didn't see you come along the Way, I kept going. I thought you might have kept walking, but when some other pilgrims said that you were looking for me in Tineo I turned around," he said.

His lips quivered as he talked, just as they did at Sundown Ranch, just before Judy tore into him for the hateful things he said to me while on drugs.

"Well, we should probably agree on a fixed meeting place from now on. I'll also give you my other phone," I said, referring to another international unlocked phone I carried. As I said this, he relaxed. His eyebrows flattened and his lips stopped quivering.

"Okay," he said, nodding in assent.

"Do you want to go get some lunch? I'm starving," I proposed.

"I'll go with you, but I'm not going to eat much. I'm still

full from anchovies and nuts."

We walked just past the Plaza in front of the City Hall and found a small restaurant, Sidreria El Refugio, nestled on the other side of the building over looking the valley below the village. Its owner, Maria, welcomed us in as if she were our mother welcoming us home to eat after a long journey. As we sat awaiting our meal, Juan entered. Donning a black trench coat, black gaucho hat, and black boot covers, and scruffy facial hair, he looked as if he were Zorro walking into the bar, tired and drenched from a long chase of bandits. The three of us enjoyed our lunch in this hidden crevasse on the outskirts of Old Town before departing.

Rain pounded us on the uphill trek to Borres, a small town of less than one hundred inhabitants with the albergue at which we planned to stay. By that point in the afternoon, all of our shoes had a thick cake of mud around the soles. When puddles blocked the trail, we didn't care any more to look for stepping stones or dry paths around them. The hike to Borres to Tineo dragged on for several hours—more than my anticipated after-lunch walk.

We arrived by early afternoon at the *albergue*—a block shaped red brick school-house looking building set on a hill some one hundred meters above the main trail. The inside of the albergue was simple but sufficient, consisting of some eight bunk beds in a rectangular room in sets of four facing each other end-to-end. Some pilgrims had arrived to stake their claim on a few of them, including Omar, his pilgrim companion Alfonso, a couple of Bavarian pilgrims we had not yet met and their Austrian traveling companion Christian.

Cory and I each laid our backpacks down on a bunk bed to stake our claim, after which I removed my foul-smelling socks to assess the damage to my aching feet. In addition to blisters on my toes, I was beginning to get horseshoe blisters on my heels. After putting on my slippers, I got up for a brief walk to survey the other facilities, only to find that other than a toilet and shower, there were none. Not that we expected it, for only by the generosity of the nearby community did we have a place to sleep, but with likely ten to fifteen pilgrims that would spend the night in a thirty by twenty foot room, we were going to have to get cozy.

That night we all sat around the radiator drinking red wine in Dixie cups. I sat on the bottom bunk of the bed near the door; Juan on a plastic chair next to the radiator, as did Omar. Cory and Alfonso stood at adjacent bunk beds. Next to the window sat a pilgrim who had arrived late day—Arturo. In his mid-fifties, Arturo was from Uruguay but had recently been granted Spanish citizenship by birthright. His grandfather was from Galicia, and he had come to explore the land of his ancestors. He started his exploration by walking the Primitive Way.

As I sat on the bed, dry and cozy in my slippers, Omar noticed the ring on my finger.

"Are you married?" he queried, in Spanish.

"Yes," I said.

"He has a son," Cory added in perfect Spanish. He could understand discrete, short questions as Omar's.

"You are so young!" Omar replied, astonished.

This was a common response I had heard in Spain when talking about marriage. When Amanda and I walked the Way four years prior, many Spaniards were astonished that we had married so young. I was twenty-three and she was twenty-one. Even at the age of twenty-seven, as I was then, he was surprised to see someone married, much less with a child.

I answered that while we were young, we were adults who had reasoned our decision for two years. We had moreover been married happily for four years without regret. Omar, then blindsided me, asking:

"Are you religious?"

All eyes were on me at this point. The mood turned somber. Perturbed by labels, I hesitated to answer. I could be Rastafarian or Russian-Orthodox and still answer 'yes,' to his question. Reflecting back to my Spanish history course from when I was in college, however, the question seemed to make more sense coming from a home-grown Spaniard from Andalucía. In the post-Ferdinand-and-Isabelle, post-Inquisition, post-Franco era of Spain, his question meant: are you a Rosary-praying, Mass-going, Saint-worshipping, Pope-loving supporter of traditional, non-heterogeneous, and orthodox society? The question, I realized, was charged.

"Well, I'm not quite sure what you mean," I said, trying to be nuanced.

"I am Catholic," I went on, not wanting to be vague, "but that's not the only reason we got married young. Our Priest never commanded us to get married. We simply made the decision that we love each other, and once we did, the next step was to consider marriage."

His face looked intrigued. My foreign-ness really became apparent. Until then, I was, it seemed to him, practically Spanish. I was speaking Spanish nearly all the time, could talk endlessly about Spanish current events or Spanish history and was freely drinking espresso and wine. I was moreover a leisurely walker—not typical of American pilgrims. After professing that I am Catholic and that I married early, however, then I seemed alien. A young Spanish person professing openly his fidelity to the Catholic Church, a church, which in Spain's post-Franco era had been seen as a bastion of everything wrong with the past, seemed too much of an anomaly to be true.

He continued to query me.

"Do you think love is possible if someone is not religious?" he asked.

"Wait a minute!" I said, with a face feigning seriousness.

"If I'm going to answer that, you'll have to pour me some more wine."

Then I said what I thought was: "Or better yet a shot"…

Until everyone gave me a strange look.

"I don't understand," Omar remarked.

"You know, like of liquor."

"Oh, you mean *chupito*?" he asked, in Spanish. "*Chupa* is something different."

As soon as everyone realized my malapropism, they uproariously laughed. I laughed too. I had meant to say the word for "a shot" (*chupito*) and accidentally said the word for "a suck" (*chupa*).

After that, the mood lightened. The bottle of La Rioja wine was passed around and we all filled our cups.

"Of course I think someone not religious can fall in love," I answered, "but I certainly would not deny that our love is related to what we believe…the idea that true love is expressed through marriage."

"Did you marry in the Church?" Omar replied.

"Of course," I said.

"Wow, so traditional."

"Possibly, though wasn't marriage in the Church quite common in Spain until recently?"

"Yes, when people were religious and believed in that. But not me, I don't believe in any of that. I'm completely atheist."

"I would think that in your parents' generation this would be less common?"

"You are right," he said.

"The problem is," Arturo from Uruguay interjected, "in my country religion has been connected to nationalism and dictatorship. In people's minds, then, religion is linked to power and authority and not to love."

The same, Juan said, was true in Spain. Politics didn't have anything to do with love.

"Look at that S.O.B Franco," he said. "He went to church on Sunday then was having his opponents killed on Monday."

"Does that mean that Franco was really Catholic?" I asked. Pope John Paul II, I mentioned, never supported Franco.[xviii]

All were silent. This was getting touchy, I could tell. We could talk about love. We could talk about politics. We could even talk about religion. Talking about Franco *and* religion, however, was off limits. Omar shifted gears.

"Well Landon, yes you are in love." He looked at Cory, standing next to me.

"Cory, what about you? Are you married?"

Up until that point Cory had been silent. He had stood next to me, trying to pay attention, but the Spanish was too quick for him to understand. He understood Omar's question, though.

"No," he replied. He didn't care to elaborate.

"Do you have a girlfriend?" he followed.

"Yes," he said, nearly expressionless. "But I'm not in love," he said. He did not care to elaborate.

We continued to discuss politics and religion like it was the weather—still thoroughly avoiding another mention of Franco. The topic of Spain's economy was brought up. Juan bemoaned the level of spending by regional governments, who were—he argued—spending more than they could afford.

"Wait a minute," Alfonso interrupted. "You can't just go changing things so fast. You have to support the people…"

Juan interrupted. I couldn't understand the response. It was too quick and nuanced for my Spanish. They continued to argue for a few minutes. I couldn't follow it all, but I got the point. Alfonso believed that austerity measures should not be so dramatic as to essentially cut people off from what they were promised. Juan countered that government spending should not come from debt that can't be paid back. In the end, Alfonso threw his arms up in the air and went to his bunk. There was no shouting. They respectfully disagreed.[xix]

Alfonso retired to his bunk on the other side of the room. Juan, Omar, Cory, Arturo and I continued to talk until we finished the wine. Exhausted, we all went to bed around ten o'clock.

I fell asleep quickly that night, only to be awoken by sounds of an F16 fighter jet flying overhead. For several minutes, I tossed and turned in bed in that foggy state of confusion about whether I was in a dream or reality, only to wake up suddenly. My heart pounded as the jet sound continued to roar, as if it were flying directly overhead. Then I looked to the bunk next to me and there lay Arturo, snoring away in peaceful slumber. I tried covering my head with a pillow, but the cacophony was too fierce. After several minutes, I stood up, crept quietly to the foot of his bed and tugged gently on his blanket. He shifted then turned for a few seconds before letting out a quiet "Hmm!" I gently whispered "you were snoring," to which he responded "oh," and turned to his side, snoring no more. I laid back down in my bunk, resting my head on my pillow in silence when he started again, this time sounding like a gas-powered lawn-mower—a harsh crescendo when the lever is pulled followed by a leveling off once the engine is running. Fully awake after the fighter jet dream, I laid awake and still for the next couple of hours, until I was back safely into my dreams.

***

Pola de Allande
April 26, 2013

The next morning met us with more rain. The forecast delivered on its promise of several more days of overcast. The way to Pola de Allande would be a wet one. I found consolation, however, in the hope for a hearty meal at the highly-recommended Nueva Allandesa located in Pola. Domingo had warned us "not to miss it."

As Cory and I trekked the green pastured hills, the menacing grey clouds above seemed to make shapes of smirking faces, mocking with delight at our unlucky weather. We took the weather as a sign not to veer off onto the Route of the Hospitals, a diversion through the wilderness that would have brought us by several historical pilgrim hostels. With no resting point in between, the Route of the Hospitals had been discouraged when there was a possibility of inclement weather. Should a snowstorm come, the possibility of being stranded would be dangerous. We decided to play it safe. Sure enough, around mid-morning a solid mix of ice and snow began to fall. Cory put on his blue plastic poncho and walked ahead, while I trod behind bundled in my brown poncho draped over my summer hat.

After passing Borres, most of the way to Pola de Allande was on the highway. Towns would occasionally interrupt bare landscape, then coated with a misty frost. A couple of times, a bar would crop up, in which I would take a break to drink an espresso, though the process of removing my rain gear took me several minutes. After the first bar, Cory ran ahead of me.

In silence, I walked along AS-219 through small towns of La Mortera, Colinas and Porciles before we arrived at the Point of Lavadoira. The word sounded like a variation of *lavadora*, the Spanish word for "washing machine." I mentioned this the night before to Omar, who had facetiously mentioned that the *Point of Secadoira*—a similar-sounding word to "drying machine"—was next.

Walking alone in the sleet, I recalled the look of fear on Cory's face the day before in Tineo. I was perplexed. Clearly bothered by our separation, he still ran ahead. There must be some other reason behind his running ahead. Maybe, I wondered, it was the cell phone I gave him. With it, perhaps he felt the liberty to continue his runs.

We caught up within an hour and arrived at Pola de Allande early in the day, despite a leisurely pace. Having been told that the 2,000 feet ascent following Pola was formidable, we decided to break for the day, after a mere 11 km hike.

The municipal albergue was nestled at the entrance to the town on highway AS-219 in an alleyway behind an apartment complex. Just behind the police station, the structure was built on a hill and elevated some 10 feet above ground on cobblestones. Its windows facing the highway were obscured by apartment structures. The sleeping area was, as in Borres, simple, with bunk beds paired up in rows in a large rectangular room. There was, however, a kitchen, and the town was within walking distance, making the place a much more ideal resting stop than last two nights' stops. We had certainly appreciated resting in the middle-of-nowhere countryside in San Juan de Villapañada and Borres, but after being battered by the elements, we were ready for some creature comforts, even if in a town of only eight hundred inhabitants.

Lunch at the Nueva Allandesa came as a much-needed rest from hiking in inclement weather. Set along the River Pola, the Nueva Allandesa[xx] is located in a beige three-story brick building in the old part of town. The bottom floor serves as a restaurant; the top two stories, a hotel. The owner, Toñin, seated us in vintage wooden chairs set around double table-clothed tables, all fully set with silverware, plates, soup bowls and two drinking glasses—one for wine and one for water. Natural light from the windows at the far end of the restaurant (from the street) was supported by multiple suspended light fixtures in the room, lending it an ambiance of civilization that we had not experienced since Madrid.

Toñin reminded me of our Uncle Stevie—a straightforward country guy who knows how to cook. Uncle Stevie took great pride in his cooking for our Christmas Eve dinners, always insisting that no one but him touch the jambalaya pot.

In short time, Toñin served us with *pote asturiano*–a soup of cabbage, potatoes, beans and sausage. This was followed by one of the most delectable plates that we had ever tried: cabbage stuffed with pork and ground local vegetables gently baked and drizzled with a mouth-watering tomato broth. We had never tried anything like it. After we had begun, Toñin came to our table and asked us if we enjoyed our meal, assuring us that if we didn't like it, he would change our plate and give us something we liked until we were full. This was, I learned, his charm tactic that made the restaurant a beloved namesake in Asturias.

As we filled our stomachs with Toñin's culinary creations, we sat in silence. Sometimes we would look at the river outside the window. Other times we would look at each other. His face bore a subtle smile.

Seeing Cory's reserved look of contentment, I was reminded of when he and I used to eat lunch at my grandfather's camp. A vacation condo of sorts built on stilts some seven miles down Blind River—a tributary of Lake Maurepas in Saint James Parish, Louisiana—the camp was our vacation home as a child. Deep in the Louisiana swamp, it offered Cory and me every boy's dream of adventures. We would spend our days there canoeing, fishing, water-skiing, and swimming. Afterwards, we would eat boiled crawfish on the camp, watching the river as we ate. As we would feast on the meaty-red tails, we would eat in silence, both too tired and hungry to talk.

After eating, I sat back in my chair and relaxed as I enjoyed nourishment of my once-empty stomach.

"So, how are your feet holding up?" I asked Cory, breaking the silence.

"Just fine, don't have any blisters," he responded.

"Lucky for you, my feet are flowering with them."

"The shoes you gave me work perfectly," he added.

I had given him a pair of my worn out Geoxx dress shoes prior to the trip, which he used to hike with. I in turn bought a new pair of shoes—poorly fitting ones at that. In the end, I ended up with the blisters as I broke them in on the Primitive Way while he wore my already broken-in footwear.

I laughed.

"Shows what I get for trying to get something new. I should have just worn my old hiking boots."

He chuckled.

"How's Benny and Amanda doing?" he asked, changing the subject.

"Well," I said, "though I haven't had much signal to talk to them."

"She's working so hard," I continued, "while taking care of Benny."

"More than I could do," he affirmed.

As we were talking Omar came in and joined us. We sat and chatted with him. Toñin came shortly. Omar ordered. Meanwhile, Toñin insisted that we try the wine. I held my glass up. Cory seemed hesitant.

"Just *un poquito*," he said.

Toñin poured us all a small amount of wine. Cory took one sip and stuck to drinking water. We stayed with Omar for a short while before heading back to the albergue. Exhausted, we laid down in our beds and rested.

Later that afternoon, I availed myself of the opportunity to go to Saturday evening Mass at the Church of Saint Andrew.[xxi] A small, gothic structure built in the sixteenth century, the Church of Saint Andrew was nearly full. For a town with a population of no more than eight hundred people, there must have been nearly twenty percent of the town at Mass that night—certainly a much higher attendance rate than the typical Spanish parish. Parishioners filed in quickly, eager to take a seat before the service began.

Rain picked up after Mass at Saint Andrew's. Dawn had set in though no sunset was visible through the clouds. As I strolled back to the *albergue*, my toes tingled. Wearing only socks and shower slippers, little separated them from the elements. I raced back to the *albergue*, some five minutes walking distance from the church.

Back at the albergue, I found Cory and Juan sitting on chairs in the make-shift living room, chatting.

"How was Mass?" Cory asked, noting my entrance.

"Good," I said, "surprised that so many showed up for such a small town."

"Anything we should visit?" Cory asked.

"There's a side chapel with a local icon, but I couldn't tell you what it's about."

"Local superstition?" Juan asked.

"Certainly a tradition," I said.

Juan then changed the subject.

"In Santiago," Juan said, knowing that I've been on the *Camino* before, "you'll tell me what to see?"

"I'll tell you what I know, but I don't think I know the city well, even having been there twice. One of my favorite sights, though, was the St James statue at the entrance—the one with the handprint beneath it."

"Though I think," I continued, "you can't place your hand on it anymore—the Cathedral's cordoned off the pillar."

"And the Cathedral, he says, how do you enter? Do you go on your knees?" he asked.

He was serious. Pious pilgrims in the Middle Ages would often enter the Cathedral on their knees, feeling unworthy to enter on their feet. I immediately thought of the movie *The Way* (2010) when Joost entered the *Portico de Gloria* on his knees. Though reverent, this scene struck me as too made-for-Hollywood. Except on film, I had never witnessed anyone entering on their knees.

I chuckled.

"Actually, I walk," I answered with a gentle sarcasm.

Cory and Juan chuckled.

At that I got up to check on our laundry, hung up on clothe-lines at the front entrance.

They were still damp.

I then peeked out the front door, hoping to find that the rain had stopped. There was still a persistent drizzle. While unfortunate, I thought, at least we had a place to stay dry for the night.

***

New York, New York

November 2010

One November Saturday morning while I was in my apartment in New York, my mom called me. She was concerned about Cory. After his bike accident, he had simply not been the same. At first he started forgetting simple things, like where he left his bike or to show up for a construction job he had promised to do. This could be a sign of falling back into addiction, she worried. Moreover, she was concerned about his decision to be homeless.

I say decision because he made an active choice. He could have lived with his girlfriend—who he had been living with—or with one of his many friends in his dance community. He even could have lived with our parents. Rather, he wanted the freedom to be alone, not work and choose when and where to lay his head down at night.

I tried to allay our mom's fears. I had recently seen Cory in October when Amanda and I visited Louisiana for my birthday. He seemed to have recovered from injuries from his bike accident. I recounted to her that he, Amanda and me had spoken at length on the car ride from Baton Rouge to Houston, where I had dropped him off to catch a bus to Austin. He adamantly insisted, I recalled, that fear was a path to negativity and should be avoided. Even when I tried to convince him to wear a bike helmet, he declined, citing fear of getting hit again as an emotion he had to face.

Homelessness, I assured my mom, was his path to face that fear. Not that I approved of his choice, I understood why he did. He was feeling off-centered by his accident. He had likely suffered a concussion, and he wanted to be alone for his recovery. The more he could embrace simplicity, the more peaceful he felt. In his estimation, divesting of most possessions, especially a home, was a path to clarity of mind. His hope was to return to a healthy, civilized life, I assured her.

She began to cry.

"I understand," she sobbed, "but it is so hard to see him out there wet and cold in the rain."

"It's ok," I said. "He is trying to do the right thing." She was comforted.

A couple of weeks after talking to my mom, Cory called me. He was in San Diego, California. He had hitched a ride to California with someone he had found on Craigslist, agreeing to pay for part of the gas. He was now sleeping on the beach in San Diego. He called me to ask if our cell phone plan—the one mom and dad had us on—would charge roaming fees in Tijuana.

"Tijuana?!" I blurted out. "Why would you want to go there?"

He told me that the hotels and food were cheap in Tijuana. He wanted shelter from the rain and didn't have money for a motel in San Diego. With the little money that he had panhandled, he could hardly afford shelter.

He wanted to come home but did not have the money to find a bus. He had tried to find another Craigslist arrangement similar to the one that brought him there, but he hadn't found one.

"Don't do that," I said. "Mexico is dangerous along the border. It's not how it used to be when mom and dad would take us to Laredo as kids. Things are much more violent. Why don't you talk to mom and dad about a plane ticket home? I'm sure they would help you."

"You don't understand," he said. "I can't do that."

I told him that I didn't know about roaming charges but begged him not to go to Mexico. He insisted that he would go.

7.
Blindsided

"One day you stepped in snow, the next in mud, water soaked in your boots and froze them at night, it was the next worst thing to pure blizzardry, it was weather that wouldn't let you settle."
— E.L. Doctorow, *Welcome to Hard Times*

Pola de Allande
April 27, 2013

Snow coated the muddy Way in the mountains outside Pola de Allande. It coated the sprouting spring foliage on a fresh, sunny April morning. The temperature was fairly warm for snow, however, reaching perhaps even 45F, which resulted in the prompt melting of the snow on my shoes. Now with fully blossomed blisters on both heels, the wetness burned. I had learned by then that not only were my new shoes waterproof, they also fit poorly. Nonetheless, the warm weather and the glistening frost-tinged Asturian Mountain-top and farmhouses had a way of alleviating the physical pain.

As we began our two-thousand foot ascent to the Puerto Palo, the snow began anew. Within an hour, several inches of snow turned into several feet. We had by then walked several miles past any sign of civilization. With no pilgrims in sight, Cory and I were left to hike this rugged mountain trail alone.

Eventually, the heavy snow turned into a blizzard. The two-foot signposts with seashells on them placed along the trail to mark the Way became obscured by fresh snow. We could not see twenty feet ahead. To find our way, we tried to make out footprints in the snow from pilgrims who had passed by earlier in the morning. At times, however, even footprints were obscured by fresh snow, and we would first walk the easiest route away from obvious drop-offs until we could see a signpost peeping out of the snow. If we didn't see one after one-hundred feet or so, we would walk back to where we were on the trail and try another path.

As visibility dropped, I had a flashback to when I watched Martin Sheen's *The Way* (2010).[xxii] This weather seemed like similar circumstances to when the doctor's son died on the ascent from Saint Jean Pied de Port. I feared that we would arrive at a similar fate and that our parents would be walking this same path on a sunny day, spreading our ashes.

Looking for some sign of comfort, I grabbed the devotional card from my backpack. Father's words came to mind—"Each day is a new *etapa.*" Glancing at the Virgen de Covadonga before placing the card in my pants pocket. I was filled with a new hope as I was reminded of all the pilgrims who sought her protection along the Primitive Way. For hundreds of years pilgrims had weathered these mountains to make it to Santiago de Compostela.

Focusing on the trail, I watched every step Cory made, making sure that there was no obvious cliffs and ravines onto which he could step. Slowly, we trekked through the wintry wilderness, trying to keep calm though we had just been blindsided.

***

New York, NY
December 06, 2010

It was a cold December morning in New York when my mom called me.

"I just heard from Cory," she said, matter-of-factly.

"And?" I asked, nervously.

My heart started to race. She wouldn't call me this early unless it was serious. Cory had not been responding to phone calls since Thanksgiving.

"He's been arrested," she said.

"What?!" I shouted. "For what?"

"The charge is human trafficking. He won't tell me more before he talks to his lawyer."

She then asked me not to tell anyone at this point. We would not tell our extended family she said. She would tell me more news as it became available. We hung up.

I did not know what to think. I was blindsided. I wondered how much worse could a charge be? When one thinks of human trafficking, one thinks of crimes against humanity. I knew Cory not to be so cruel as to enslave someone. Yet knowing that he—my brother—was arrested and charged with such a crime could not keep me from wondering what exactly happened. I felt frightened, on one hand, at his prospects. Would he spend the rest of his life incarcerated? Worse, I felt ashamed, that my own brother was now implicated in such a heinous crime.

As I rode the van to my clinical rotation that day, I shifted nervously between looking out the window and journaling. I tried anything to forget the morning's news. Thinking about imprisonment could quickly turn into unhealthy rumination. Yet even on the van ride, I couldn't avoid reminders. Driving North on FDR drive from Manhattan to White Plains, I could make out across the East River, Roosevelt Island—once a prison. Seeing this, I turned to reading Walker Percy. I was reading *The Moviegoer* (1961) on my rides. Yet Percy's nostalgic description of Southeast Louisiana in 1960's reminded me of back at my parent's home in Baton Rouge—the last place I was with Cory.

When I got to my rotation, then I really couldn't avoid reminders of my brother. I was on my psychiatry rotation at New York Presbyterian Hospital in Westchester —an inpatient psychiatric hospital—placed on the substance abuse floor. Day in and day out, I worked with patients whose lives had been ruined by addiction, a possibility my brother was now facing.

Several days after hearing news of my brother, I remember accompanying the psychiatrists to court where they would testify to a patient's need for further institutionalization—against his or her will. Seeing the looks of shame on a patient's face as the judge remanded them to the mental hospital pierced my heart. Even though I agreed with the judge—that the patient was not safe to live in the community—it pained me to know that my own brother would soon be in a similar spot, brought before a judge and told that he was not safe to live in society. I felt ashamed. No matter how much I tried to avoid it, I could not avoid reminders of my brother's incarceration.

***

Puerto del Palo, Asturias
April 27, 2013

After reaching the highest point of the day, Puerto Palo, the snow slowed to an eventual stop. We made it safely through the rugged mountain terrain to the highway. There were several signposts with shells along highway, indicating continuation of the Way off of the highway. After our trail-finding fiasco, however, we stayed on the highway. We walked for several miles before arriving at the town of Berducedo, a small town of no more than two-hundred inhabitants, situated right on the highway.

We stopped in the first bar, which turned out to be the only one. There we found Juan sitting at the bar eating a sandwich. After talking with the owner and some town residents, we learned that the next *albergue* in La Mesa was equipped with no more than a single room with beds. Moreover there was nowhere to eat in the twenty-person town. After the conditions we had faced earlier that day, we decided to stop for the day in the municipal albergue of Berducedo, whose *hospitalera*, Marcelina, happened to be in the bar.

Much like Borres, the *albergue*, located in an old schoolhouse building, had a simple feel. With six double bunk beds situated in three rows, the place looked like a smaller replica of the former. There was also a basic kitchen area for preparing food though cooking was not an option. After claiming our beds, we all took turns showering to warm water—thankfully. Omar arrived shortly after Juan, Cory and me, followed by Arturo. In the evening, I availed myself of some wine, cheese and sausage, which Cory cut and prepared for us. We spent the rest of the evening sitting around the table drinking wine, eating cheese, and sharing snow stories. This time, we did not talk religion or politics.

***

Castro, Asturias
April 28, 2013

By the time we woke up in Berducedo the next day, much of the snow had melted. The town of La Mesa came quickly after we began our walk. After La Mesa the elevation began to rise, dampening our pace. The snow had altogether ceased but had left in its wake a twenty mile-per-hour wind that cut through our skin as we hiked up the wind-side of the mountain. Cory and I walked in silence along the country road some five-hundred feet higher in elevation to the top of a windmill-lined hill. The shielding from the other side of the mountain could not come soon enough.

He walked ahead of me for most of the climb. Sometimes, however, I would catch up and walk alongside him. At other times, however, I would slow down and walk behind him—though always in talking distance. Cory trekked steadily with a bullish determination. Once I had to stop and catch my breath.

I was incredulous. I was always the athletic one. He quit T-Ball when he was six or seven, while I played baseball until I was fifteen and high school basketball—albeit for a short while. Now, he was the one who was better withstanding the physical challenge. Yet it wasn't just his fitness that I couldn't believe. He was now—after prison—pure muscle and bone—just as he was when he was on drugs in high school. But now, he struck me as a bulky but gentle teddy bear, insisting on cuddling in the park with my son Benny when he came to Houston from San Diego.

After a painstaking climb, we came to the top, finding a town called Buspol, outside of which was a small chapel, the Chapel of Saint Mary of Buspol.[xxiii] Cory and I stopped briefly to enjoy the shelter from the wind before continuing our ascent.

Just beyond Buspol, the view of the Salime Reservoir came into view. The reservoir houses a 123 foot-high gravity dam, which generates hydro-electric power from the melted snow running off the mountains.[xxiv] Still several miles off, now no longer assaulted by the wind, we began our descent to this emerald lake nestled in the mountains. When we arrived at the bottom, the trail met back up with the same highway kept us on the path to Berducedo the day before. The highway brought us over the dam and across the reservoir to the embankment on the other side, where the town of Grandas de Salime lie some six kilometers away. As usual, we did not come across a single soul during the day's trek.

Thankfully, however, only a mile past the dam we came upon Hotel Las Grandas,[xxv] a hotel-restaurant built along the mountainside over-looking the reservoir. Juan was there waiting for us, while Omar had already gone ahead to Grandas. We all ordered coffee and sat on the veranda overlooking the reservoir, hoping to enjoy the view of the mountain range we had just crossed. We didn't stay there for long, however, for in crossing the dam, we had returned to the receiving end of the fierce wind. We moved indoors, where it was warmer and the wind didn't assault us.

Seated comfortably next to the window, Cory and I sipped our coffees while Juan read the newspaper. After a few minutes, Cory went to the restroom. I sat back in my chair to admire the view from beyond the veranda. Down below, the emerald-green reservoir glistened.

Above, the mountains we had just crossed towered. For a moment, I felt accomplished, but then, thinking of Cory, feelings of victory were tempered. We had endured downpours, a blizzard and biting winds as we climbed higher in elevation, but I couldn't bring myself to believe that Cory and I were accomplishing the same ground in our relationship. After our first day of walking together, he was running ahead for parts of our hike. It bothered me that I couldn't figure out why.

***

Houston, TX

January 2011

In January of my third year of medical school, I got a short break from the New York winter. One Friday morning I woke up to several feet of snow along East 77th Street. I took a flight that day to Houston. There the weather was sunny and cool—though not cold—and the oaks still had green leaves.

I went to Houston to be with my wife Amanda and my father-in-law. He had broken his leg the previous December and eventually lost circulation to the bottom of the leg, requiring amputation and an eventual prosthetic. Amanda stayed by his side during the surgery and recovery process. I had seen her little during the foregoing two months and had not visited her father since he broke his leg.

During that trip, I also saw my mother, who visited my

father-in-law en route to her home in Baton Rouge. As I learned from her, Cory was indeed guilty of a crime. While homeless in San Diego, a professional smuggler approached him. Termed coyotes, professional smugglers are known to prey on homeless in San Diego, often times luring them from shelters and soup kitchens, offering them help while they are desperate. Cory was offered cash in exchange for driving an immigrant across the border in a van. Desperate to secure finances to return home, he took up the offer. He reasoned that while he was committing a crime, he was potentially solving two problems while not directly hurting anyone: giving access to better work and living conditions to an immigrant and giving himself the chance to return home to be with his family. He was not interested in making money.

At the border checkpoint, he was caught by Customs and Border Patrol agents who used infrared sensors and human sniffing dogs. He was arrested and imprisoned at the Metropolitan Correctional Center (MCC) in San Diego. His trial and sentencing would not happen until April. He had agreed to plead guilty in hopes of a lesser sentence.

Before the judge would sentence him, he would review his sentencing memorandum—a compendium of letters and affidavits from friends and family attesting to who Cory was as a person. This could be used to lessen his sentence length. Though a massive campaign of Facebook—"Cory's Support Group"—our mom began to assemble an extensive memorandum. My mom had traveled to Austin to collect letters of support from Cory's friends there to build his memorandum—friends who knew him to be kind-hearted and incapable of committing a crime with ill will.

The news of my brother's attempt to transport an immigrant across the US-Mexico border—though a naive and impulsive action—quelled my shock over his arrest and charges with "human trafficking." While guilty of the alleged charge, the term "human trafficking' was far too imprecise to describe the complexity surrounding his decision to commit a crime. Until that point, the mere knowledge of my brother's incarceration for "human trafficking" left me with fear that he would find himself severely punished by society and leave our family ostracized for a charge whose magnitude only falls short of "human rights abuse." I was blindsided by his arrest, but now that I knew the details surrounding his crime, I was consoled. I returned to New York from Houston hopeful about Cory that the judge would—after reading his memorandum—grant him a lenient sentence. Maybe, Cory would learn to temper the impulsive behaviors that got him into trouble in the first place.

8.
Shedding Excess Baggage

I don't believe in a lot of baggage. It's such a nuisance. Life's too short to fuss with it. And it isn't really necessary
— Hugh Lofting, *The Voyages of Doctor Dolittle*

After nearly a week of walking the Way, one skill that I learned to refine by then was packing my backpack. With every extra pound causing more soreness and fatigue at the day's end, I learned to minimize weight to alleviate pains in my shoulders and chest. Every morning after breakfast I would go through every pocket of my bag, questioning whether its contents were useful for the journey or whether they could be left behind or thrown away. Such was the fate of the flint and steel. (After the six-course meal from Casa Pachón, I realized that we wouldn't be needing to cook our meals over open fire.) Occasionally, I would have to pick up contents along the way, such as a bar of soap with which to wash our laundry over each *albergue's* washing sink. At least once per day, I would do a mental run-through of my backpack pockets, trying to figure out how to assuage my burden and make the way more bearable.

As I refined the process of subjecting my backpack to daily purging, I realized that the process was not only external but also internal. Amid the stillness of the walk and the simplicity of the daily rhythm, I would find moments throughout the day to reflect on thought patterns I carried with me. When a strong feeling was evoked, walking was an opportunity to reflect on where the feeling came from, why might I have felt it and whether it was a feeling to hold onto or just let go.

This was the case with drinking coffee at bars along the Way the first time I walked it with Amanda. My avoidance was linked to my anxiety over my brother. I was afraid of becoming an addict like him—letting substances cripple my life and veer me off course. Drinking coffee along the Way with Amanda helped me let go of my excessive fears of becoming an addict. This time, I drank it in a much healthier manner than when I used it to stay up late and study.

This was also the case with the urge I felt to check my phone for text messages or emails when passing an Orange store in Grado. While walking, I thought of all the times since I got a phone that I pulled out my phone just to check for a message with no real goal in mind. I thought of all the minutes that I spent on my phone that could have been paired down while still allowing me to accomplish the same goals. I thought of all the times that I spent on my phone that could have been spent writing in my journal, or better, writing letters to loved ones. Then I realized how—after getting a smart-phone nine months prior—I had fallen prey at times to letting technology rule me, and not letting myself rule it. I resolved to develop a healthier phone interaction, to be more deliberate with technology that is at my fingertips.

As I walked with Cory along the highway past Grandas, the rain picked up. I felt for a moment disappointment. The usual three days of inclement weather was tarrying, and I felt as if the weather should follow the forecast, which for several days had predicted the sun would come out "tomorrow." Then I would be forced to grapple with the fact that weather does not conform to forecasts.

I was also feeling sorry for Cory. We had just stopped for lunch at Grandas, and Cory, not wanting to order, agreed to sit with me. Mid-way through the meal, he ordered a small plate of cheese, thinking it would cost him only 5€, as he later told me. When the check came, he was surprised to find it cost 12€. Flustered, he tried to explain to the waitress that he wouldn't have bought the plate had he known the price.

"*No sabía que cuesta doce euros*," he said in his Tex-Mex Spanish. ("I didn't know it cost twelve euros.")

As he tried to further dispute the charge, I stopped him. I insisted on paying the tab. He accepted, but I could tell he felt apprehensive receiving my help. As he had told me in Madrid, he wanted to pay me back for every penny I spent on him.

When we arrived at the *albergue* in Castro, however, I forgot about the incident. This stone-built cottage was sleek and homey—less rustic and threadbare than the ones before. It had a restaurant, bar, hardwood floors, smaller rooms of four beds each, and free Wi-Fi. Unlike the previous municipal *albergues*, which were managed by community volunteers, it was a private, youth *albergue*, which was run by a seasonal worker who would tend to the place during the spring and summer. Thankfully, though, we not only found the only comfortable place for many miles ahead but our friends Omar, Juan and Alfonso had already arrived, with Arturo, as usual, on his way.

That night Cory and I joined Omar, Alfonso and Arturo at the *albergue*'s eatery. After a full lunch in Grandas, Cory and I decided to forego dinner. As we joined them in conversation, Omar grabbed the bottle of wine next to him and offered to pour Cory and me a glass.

"Sure," I said. Cory declined.

I then asked Arturo where he was sleeping. He pointed to one of the corners above, where the sleeping rooms were situated.

"I know what you are thinking," he said with a wide grin. "You don't want to listen to the melodies of my snores."

"You said it," I replied.

We all snickered, Arturo included.

Cory then got up to scan the board games stacked up in the corner. He asked if anyone wanted to play. Unable to find any takers, he found a piece of paper and sat down in a chair by himself. Several minutes later he came back with an intricately folded Moravian paper star.

When he came and sat down near us again, I recalled our laundry, which had likely completed their cycle in the washer. I got up and went outside. As I pulled out our clothes and hung them up on the clothes-line, I realized that laundry was becoming my regular chore. What, I wondered, was Cory's? I couldn't think of one.

I wasn't bothered though. I was going to do my laundry anyways. He had always been somewhat unconcerned with laundry. I recall how as children, I would meticulously pick up my dirty clothes from by bedroom and put them in the hamper, while he would plot with my sister how he could position dirty clothes on the floor so as to fluster our meticulously clean mother.

The following day the Way from Castro was the wettest one so far. Rain pounded us as we walked along the highway. Occasionally the cars passing by would splash us. Added to that was a misty fog that made visibility less than perfect. My hopes were not down, however, for I resolved to believe the forecast, which predicted several days of sun, even if it was only to keep my hopes up. Cory, Juan and I walked together for the first part of the morning until I, lured by an open bar along the Way, stopped for respite from the elements. Cory, as usual, continued on, while Juan joined me.

Walking in with a cloak-like poncho into this dimly lit bar with wooden tools hung on the walls and old vintage wines hung on wooden racks above the bar, I felt as if I were a Hobbit stumbling into a tavern in the Shire. As we sat at the bar, Juan asked the bartender what was available to eat. The bartender, an old gentleman with a small pot-belly and a thick Astur-Galician accent, pointed to a plate at a nearby table with four or five pieces of sliced sausage and cheese. He then nodded, looking at us like we were just supposed to get it. Juan pressed on, asking "how much does a plate like that cost?"

He replied, "Oh, a plate like that cost five euros."

Juan, infuriated by his curtness, promptly said "*Hasta luego*," donned his Zorro-looking trench coat and left. I stayed behind to have an espresso, which, after another night of another night if Arturo's snoring—audible even through the walls of another room in Castro—I needed. Sitting at a table in front of the bar was a middle-aged couple, clearly—evidenced by their backpacks and raingear—both pilgrims. We began to chat. Speaking in Spanish, they were from Argentina, they told me. They asked where I was from—a common question I would get from Spanish speakers along the Way. My Spanish, while clearly not native-sounding, does not sound Anglo either, leaving many Spanish speakers confused as to where I am from. I told them that I was from the US and that I was traveling with my brother, who walked ahead of me that morning. The woman responded that she had heard of us.

"Oh yes, you are one of the *Hermanos Tejanos*," she said. ("The Texan Brothers.")

I was surprised that anyone outside of our small clan that

we would see each day knew who we were, much less where we came from. They recounted that they had stayed in hotels part of the time, perhaps accounting for our not having met until that point. They moreover said that other pilgrims had spoken of us. Cory was said to be like a bull, able to run fast, carry his backpack and never tire. Not wanting to lag far behind Cory, I bid adieu from our chat, donned my poncho, and exited the tavern on the shire.

Outside I marched on through the rain. The first half of the way was another uphill climb. I wasn't bothered however—not even by the rain. Rain had become the norm, as had uphill climbs. Plus the sun was coming.

After about twenty kilometers of hiking in the pouring rain, I stumbled upon an oasis. Famished after a simple breakfast at Castroverde, the Meson Catro Vientos lie right along the Way en route to the next major town of Fonsagrada. A two-story Galician style cottage of natural stone and vintage wood, the eatery boasted a clean, smooth interior with wooden furniture and a warm fire for heating. Within minutes I was sitting on the second-floor gallery next to the window overlooking the way in a quiet, empty room.

The view of the Galician hills, I imagined, looked better when the rain had gone. I thought of where Cory might be. Staring out the window at the rainy hills, I surmised that he was probably somewhere ahead, soaking wet. Turning my gaze back to the table, I looked at the empty seat across from me. Just then I felt—for a moment—

empty. I wanted to share this experience with Cory, who by then had walked too far ahead.

After a short time, lunch was served.

Mid-way through the meal another gentleman was brought into the room by the waiter. He was a middle-aged English-speaking pilgrim—at least I presumed from the accent he had when he said *gracias*. I asked him to join me. Sure enough, he was American. His name was Ray, and he was a Catholic Priest of the Redemptorist Order. In fact, he was the order's former Secretary General. Ironically, we had several Redemptorist Priest friends in common. When my wife and I lived in New York, we had a tradition of going to a Valentine's day retreat at Mount Saint Alphonsus—a Medieval castle-looking former Redemptorist seminary along the Hudson, not far from West Point.[xxvi] We had gotten to know a couple of priests there over the years.

After enjoying my peaceful meal with Ray, I said goodbye and went downstairs to pay. Running short on cash, I asked to pay with credit card, which had been advertised as accepted. The owner, Ovidio, graciously attempted to run my card, which for some reason kept returning receipts saying "not accepted." Despite multiple attempts the card came back as rejected though I had successfully used it in Pola de Allande. Ovidio, embarrassed, showed me the receipt, saying, "I'm not sure if it went through." Eventually, he got frustrated, saying "It's okay. Don't worry about it." Having seen each transaction as denied, however, I knew that he wouldn't get his money if I didn't pay him in cash, so I paid him with my dwindling supply of euros. For twelve euros, I couldn't have asked for more. I would get cash at the next ATM.

As I walked along the soppy trail after lunch, I realized that with the exception of Pola de Allande—which I explicitly offered to pay for—Cory ate dinner and breakfast at albergues but never lunch along the Way. It occurred to me as well that he had mentioned in conversation they day before that that he was concerned about having enough cash to finish the trip. Cory's only method of payment was the 180€ I had given him in Madrid. After being released from prison, he had not managed to acquire a credit card.

Then I realized why he had been running ahead during lunch-time.

He knew that I liked to stop for pilgrim's menus mid-day and, not wanting to put me in the position to have to pay for him, would avoid the occasion to put me on the spot. It was also why he was stopping in the municipal *albergues*, which charged either donation or a few euros. Even when I wanted to pay for him, he accepted sparingly. While I would have gladly paid for a meal together, he spurned financial help. Still, I wanted my brother there, even if it cost me twelve euros. I vowed from then on that I would insist on paying for his meals. Nothing could buy back the time we were spending together.

I met back up with Cory at the municipal *albergue* of Padrón, located some two kilometers past the town of Fonsagrada along the highway. The white, two-story house with a natural-stone finished bottom housed six rooms, each with two sets of bunk beds. The bottom floor held a kitchenette and entry foyer, which connected to the top by creaky, old wooden stairs. Our friends Juan, Omar and Alfonso stayed in Fonsagrada.

With rain still lingering outside and nowhere to go for two kilometers, Cory and I took the evening time inside. With a clearer cell-phone signal, I was able to contact my wife Amanda and son Benny. My father-in-law was taking care of Benny, who was crying in the absence of his mother, despite Fred's every attempt to pacify him with a bottle and clean diaper. Hearing his cry was heart-wrenching, for I desperately wanted to hold and comfort him. My dear wife, Amanda, meanwhile, was at work. I called her immediately afterwards. She spoke to me from the closet given to her to pump milk during breaks. She told me that she missed me, as I did her. We didn't have long to chat, however, for even in her off-period she had people to meet with and papers to grade. After speaking with her, I went down to the foyer to join Cory, as he practiced Spanish with the recent arrivals.

Rain lingered on the day we departed from Padrón. The forecast seemed to keep predicting sun for the next day. The Way crisscrossed with a rural road as we traversed muddy pastures filled with cattle, now quite wet from the week's downpour. After a short seven kilometers we came across ruins of a stone wall, a cobble-stoned road and a house-like structure overgrown with lichens and vegetation. It was the Royal Hospital of Montouto. Built in the 1300s, the hospital was known to house pilgrims, who, according to one pilgrim's account in 1856, "suffered from cold and snow." The hospital functioned as an albergue for nearly six centuries before falling into ruins. Beside the ruins lie a simple chapel, erected more recently, offering just enough shelter for Cory and I to take a break from the rain before moving on.

Cory walked not far ahead of me until I along with Juan, who we had crossed paths with that morning, who we had crossed paths with that morning, decided to stop for coffee in Casa Meson in the town of Paradavella. A two-story, stone-built house with a patio and two picnic tables in front—which made great resting spots for our backpacks—Casa Meson was another homegrown oasis in the midst of the rural Primitive Way. Juan and I seated ourselves and ordered a coffee from Antonio, the owner. The only clients present at the time, Juan and I had the chance to speak with Antonio, its owner, as he swept the floor. A short, thin man with black-rimmed glasses, a grey goatee and a beanie covering the rest of his head, he did not look like the typical Galician. Indeed, he had emigrated from Argentina more than twenty years ago, bought the house—in some degree of ruin at the time—restored it and turned it into a restaurant, bar and residence for pilgrims along the Way. Juan, curious how a new business had done in recent times, asked how he had weathered "the crisis," to which Antonio said that while difficult, he would keep on doing what he loves.

After a refreshing cup of Antonio's coffee, we continued in the rain, en route to the next closes *albergue* along the Way, the municipal *albergue* of Cadavo Baleira. The *albergue*, perhaps among the most comfortable ones that we had since stayed at, bore an odd design. The main building—a white, block shaped structure—contained the sleeping rooms and entry hall, while a rather odd metallic addition held the bathrooms. Cory and I arrived together—having met up later in the day—while Juan came later. Only present when we arrived was the Argentinean couple. Not long afterwards, Juan, Alfonso, Omar and of course Arturo arrived.

By the end of the day Cory and I were famished and decided to go for a meal at the town's nicest restaurant—La Moneda. Juan, Alfonso, Omar and Arturo all joined. The rain by late evening had subsided, making for a pleasant walk to the restaurant-hotel. The temperature had dropped to the low forties, however, making my sock-covered toes tingle as I longed for my hiking boots on the radiator. Fortunately, we arrived at La Moneda after only a short walk from the *albergue* to the heated front bar. The waitress led us behind the bar to an empty dining room filled with set tables, all double-clothed. There, in short time, we were served our choice of Galician soup, tripe stew with chickpeas or Russian salad and fish, steak or chicken, a delectable array of desserts—flan, in my opinion, the best—and most importantly, house wine, which we all drank a glass, even Cory.

Drinking with Cory had always made me unsettled, for obvious reasons. The last I could recall him having alcohol in his hands before this trip the family Christmas trip to Cancún while he and I were in college. When we were walking around downtown, he snuck away to buy a bottle of rum. While I believed that it is possible for an alcoholic to learn to moderate—albeit few actually do—I always worried that alcohol would become as precious to him as Tolkien's ring was to Bilbo in *The Hobbit.* He could have a bit of it for a while, but eventually, I worried, he would reach a breaking point where he needed it above and beyond the wellbeing of all others. Then it would come to rule him, and he would whither away in selfish overconsumption of his precious and lose his social ties from all around him.

That night, however, something was different. I kept a close eye on how much he drank. He did not even finish a whole glass. I, on the other hand, drank nearly half a bottle…more than usual. This time I drank more than he did for a change.

***

Taizé, France
August 26, 2011

After my third year of medical school, I took a leave-of-absence to pursue a master's degree in Europe. Prior to beginning to graduate school, however, I had yet to take Step 1 of my US Medical Licensing Exam (USMLE)—the first step to medical licensure in the United States. Given that I was already going to Europe for my studies, I opted to take the test there. This was permitted by the international testing service that administers the exam. Prior to taking the test, I planned an intensive five-week study regimen.

In order to accomplish my study objectives, I decided to study for the test in a *gîte*—a rural house in France designated as a vacation home. I found a *gîte* in Taizé, a small village in the Burgundy mountains of France. This village, I reasoned, offered me distance from big-city distractions to focus on my studies, and it also allowed me to attend prayer services with the Taizé brothers. Started by Brother Roger after World War II, the community of Taizé is an ecumenical group of brothers who lead daily prayers in the form of simple, multilingual songs in efforts to foster peace and reconciliation between different religions and cultures. People from every religion and all over the world come to participate in their services and—if they wish—participate in week-long retreats. During the retreats, people camp in tents nearby while attending daily prayer services in the church in Taizé—now expanded to house thousands of people—while attending daily services, participating in multilingual workshops and volunteering in food-preparation.

Knowing that I would not be able to participate in the weeklong retreat, I rented a nearby *gîte* that offered me the proximity to still attend daily prayer services. The *gîte* was a rustic, several hundred year-old house midway up the hillside on which Taizé sits.[xxvii] It offered me the perfect place to study while preparing for a grueling medical licensing exam. The only drawback, however, was that it did not have internet. This was an issue when I tried to use online test preparation services.

It was also an issue when I realized that it was Cory's birthday on August 22. When I did, I composed him an email, but was unable to send it to him for two days. I finally sent it to him when I found Wi-Fi at a café in a nearby town. In it, I wished him a happy birthday, apologizing for my belated message, and suggested that we spend some time together in Baton Rouge. A couple of days later, I went back to the café and checked my email again.

He replied:

"It's okay. The message I sent to the rest of the family was:

> *On August 31 I'm having myself admitted to the Hope Center in Marksville, LA for a 28 day substance abuse rehab. I ask for no gifts on my birthday but support in this endeavor.*

I'm very sad to say, it may not be possible to see you while you are here because of the bad timing of this. There are visitations on Sunday, but unfortunately it's also two hours away from Baton Rouge."

Heartbroken by this news, I struggled to keep up my intense study regimen or Step 1 while childhood fears of my brother's demise to alcohol and drugs brewed within. Deeply perturbed and in need of support, I found consolation at the evening prayer service at Taizé. During the evening services, Catholic Priests who are visiting the community sit in chairs in a cordoned off area of the sanctuary and hear confessions. Desperate for a listening ear to express my grief about my brother's relapse, I went to the area and asked around for an English-speaking priest. I was ready to share my grief. I was directed to the Archbishop of Hartford, CT,[xxviii] who happened to be hearing confessions that night.

I told him that I did not want to make a confession, but I just needed to talk to someone about my brother.

"I just found out today that my brother relapsed on drugs and alcohol, and I'm scared..."

As the words "drugs" and "brother" left my mouth in the same sentence I began to sob. Burying my head into my hands, I said:

"Ever since he started to have problems, I've always worried that he would fall prey to his addiction and would never come back."

I wept.

He placed his warm, fatherly hand on my shoulder.

"Now, now. What's your brother's name?" he asked.

"Cory."

"Well, Cory is lucky to have a brother who cares for him as much as you do. Why don't I pray for him?"

Later that night when I returned to my *gîte*, I wrote Cory a letter. I told him that I believed in him. I expressed hope in him that even if he fell down, he would one day get up. Even if he fell one hundred times, I said, he would one day he would get up and stay up.

Cory did not share the share the same hope in himself however. When my sister and I made he trip to Marksville two week later, Cory was quite down on himself. As we ate lunch in the visiting area of this pink colonial-era house converted into drug and alcohol rehab, Cory's face bore total despair.

“I just don't see any way of recovery. Everything I have tried has failed. The only way that any true alcoholic has overcome addiction is by spiritual conversion, and I just don't see how that is going to happen when my childhood belief system has been dismantled.”

***

Cadavo Baleira

May 2, 2013

Before beginning the day’s journey from Cadavo, I did something different in my packing routine. While at the albergue in Cadavo, I took the clothespins from my backpack and pinned my wet shirt, towel, and socks to the exterior. They had failed to fully dry in the damp air of the Cadavo albergue.

That day, we were supposed to have sun, the waiter said at the Bar La Moneda. I believed it.

As we began our ascent from Cadavo up the muddy but green mountainside, Cory stopped briefly.

"Wait a minute," he interjected.

I stopped as well, thinking he must have left something behind.

"That Argentinean couple, did they sleep in the room across from us?"

"Yes" I said, wondering why it mattered.

"Aw man, they gamed us into all sleeping in one room."

"What do you mean?" I asked.

"They were the only ones in the bunkroom when I went in, but when I asked if there were any beds there, they said the room was occupied. I thought maybe other people were there but had already came by, but when I checked in the morning, only they slept there while all of us were asleep in one room."

I hadn't thought of it, but he was right. They had convinced all the other pilgrims—perhaps ten of us—that their room was full so they could have their own suite. This would not have mattered much to me were it not for the fact that I was forced to sleep in a bunk close to Arturo, whose snores inevitably woke me for at least an hour during the night.

"That is pretty annoying," I said, echoing his sentiment. He shook his head and kept walking. He was rightly frustrated—angered even—that communal resources—an *albergue*—were commandeered for private use. This was not in the pilgrim spirit of sharing sparse comforts. Frustrated, we kept walking. We quickly for got about what happened at the Cadavo *albergue*. The day was a new day. We had no other choice but to forgive.

***

Baton Rouge, Louisiana
2011

After Cory's stay at rehab in Marksville, Louisiana, he returned to my parent's house, where—per his sentencing agreement—he was under house arrest. He began drinking again and doing drugs, regularly failing urine drug screenings, testing positive for cocaine and marijuana. He was free from federal prison but not free from bondage. He had reached rock-bottom in his life while under custody of the Federal probation system. While under house arrest, his anger at his probation officer's, prison guards, US Marshalls fueled a downward spiral. Though free from the bars of Federal prison, he was after his initial release, "owned" as he was told by the prison system, an arrangement that sorely went against his roaming, free-spirited lifestyle for the previous decade. He was moreover enraged by the tactics of the parole officer's deterministic declaration that—based on a multiple choice test he was given—he stood a seventy percent chance of going back to jail. With his movements tracked with an ankle brace and his work activity restricted by the parole office, he sought consolation in drinking and drugs—a clear violation of his probation terms. When threats of revocation of his probation did not seem to dissuade him, he was moved from my parent's home to the halfway house in Baton Rouge, where he would "shift from guitar to… Wii…*ad nauseum*."

Then one day, he woke up and decided to change.

I don't know whether it was lessons from Sunday school on the Beatitudes or an intuitive sense that his anger was crippling his recovery, but lying in his bed in that dilapidated half-way house, he decided that he would forgive. He let go of all anger towards his probation officer, the US Marshalls, the prison guards and the justice system. He realized that each of them were genuinely trying to do their job in a broken criminal justice system, one into which he happened to fall into after an imprudent act of desperation. He realized that no individual committed any injustice against him, but that the problem lay with the system, one that he could only hope to change by setting an example of forgiveness and of peace. More importantly, he was able to forgive himself. His own sense of despair—that self-doubt he expressed to me when I visited him at Marksville—had always kept him from taking that step forward into recovery.

Unfortunately, as he would tell me, "the wheels of my revocation had already begun to turn by that point." Not long afterwards did US Marshall's come into the halfway house to inform him that he would be brought to the courthouse "the easy way or the hard way: You can gather your belongings peacefully and we can take you to the courthouse, or we can throw your shit away, break every tooth in your skull and still take you to the courthouse." Needless to say, he went along peacefully to the courthouse.

***

Outside Lugo, Galicia

May 2, 2013

After hiking several hundred feet up to the point of Vaqueriza, we were again met with more clouds covering up the new-found sunshine. Thankfully, though, the rain was absent. The ascent leveled off before the Way quickly descended to Lugo. The clouds stayed just long enough to shelter us from the morning heat and then abated in the afternoon. A drop did fall once or twice from the sky, but it was, thank heavens, just a couple of drops. Together, Cory and I traversed green pastures and lightly shaded forests as we inched closer to the Primitive Way's first major city.

At about eight kilometers from Cadavo we came upon Castroverde, a town of 2,000 inhabitants. A gothic structure of old stone now covered with lichen, the Cathedral of Santa Maria stands just outside the entrance to town with practically no population around it. The Medieval structure was bordered in the front by five tall semi-circular arches. Cory, not wanting to get too far ahead on the journey to Lugo, was more than willing to stop to admire this fifteenth century national monument. Inside, lie a silent, empty temple, adorned at the front by a Baroque altarpiece depicting Saints Mary, Joseph, John the Baptist and James the Moor-killer. The latter bore a figure of Saint James, marked by the seashell and pilgrim hat, seated on a horse brandishing a sword amidst a slain Arab. On the way out, I commented to Cory that in larger cities the Arab figures beneath Saint James the Moore-killer were—after the bombing of Madrid's rail station Atocha on March 11—covered with flowers, lending the statues a new name, Saint James the Gardener. He shook his head. The enshrinement of conquest did not sit well with him.

The rest of the day we spent walking through another flat twenty kilometers through green farmlands, which were interspersed multiple gullies and streams. At times, Cory and I were silent, just walking in each other's presence. We had, it was clear, a peace with each other, one that we had not shared in our adult lives, a peace in which words did not need to fill the gap that each other's presence did. At other times, we chatted. I noted a number of dilapidated, abandoned farm-houses that could—with low cost, a few raw materials and some man-power—be transformed into beautiful historic *albergues.* He concurred, expressing the hope that he could join in me in such a dream once he settled his debts. We knew that such a dream was for both of us along way off, if at all possible, but the hope of bringing out of ruins a place to sleep for pilgrims on the Primitive Way—much like Alejandro did at Bodenaya—did not keep us from dreaming.

By early afternoon, my laundry had dried. I took off the towels, shirts and socks, folded them up and put them in my bag. They were clean and dried; the excess water weight, evaporated. My backpack shed of excess items, I walked with a light burden, energized by the sun that had come up as we reached outside Lugo.

As I folded clean laundry, placed it into my backpack and put it on my back, I realized that it was my turn to shed excess baggage. I realized that my worries about Cory's drinking were part of the excess baggage with me that I had carried for over a decade. I let fear get in the way of our relationship. It was not a healthy concern for my brother's well-being but a crippling worry about our future, so much so that it stopped me from enjoying the time I had with him. It was time to let that worry evaporate and to enjoy the precious now we had together. None of us are guaranteed a future with our loved ones. If we don't cherish moments with them for what they are, we risk not cherishing our loved ones for who they are but rather who we want them to be. When I realized that all Cory wanted was for me to live with him now—the burden of our past felt much lighter. Cory had shed his excess baggage while in prison, now it was my turn.

9.
A Change Of Scenery

"There is a time for everything; a season for every activity under the heavens."
—Ecclesiastes 3:1

Lugo, Galicia
May 2, 2013

By the time we reached the outskirts of Lugo, the sun was shining in all its brilliance. As we descended to the valley outside of the city to the River Rato—the river that forms part of the moat around the city walls—massive forty-five-foot-high walls became visible. No longer guided by a single trail or roadside as the only path to take, we relied on *flechas* and *conchas* to guide as we strolled the city side-walks. Occasionally, we would come to a traffic intersection where neither a *flecha* nor *concha* was apparent. Then we would have to stop, look around and find one before moving on.

Eventually the Way led us to a gate in the city's walls.[xxix] A twelve-foot wide walkway leading through the wall and into the town's center, the Gate of Saint Peter has served as the point of entry for pilgrims for over a thousand years. As we approached the gate, we came to a crosswalk. Around the wall a modern, asphalted road circumscribed the old city—aptly named *Ronda de la Muralla* ("Rounding of the Wall"). Cars and buses zoomed by as we waited for the walk signal. Hearing them, I felt displaced. Up until then, the Way had been, as described, primitive. It now felt odd not being in a quiet countryside. Then I realized that this was the first major city we had crossed since Oviedo.

After crossing the crosswalk, we came to the gate, beside which lay an engraving inaugurating the Way of King Alfonso II—said to be the "first pilgrim"—in the ninth century.[xxx] We stopped briefly to read the inscription before crossing the gate, coming onto a narrow stone road lined with storefronts and restaurants. The old town was filled with throngs of pedestrians, none of which appeared to be pilgrims. It was Friday, the beginning of a sunny weekend, and many were out to shop and eat.

As we walked down the road, I scanned the city street for the nearest *flechas* or *conchas*, trying to keep focused on finding the albergue.[xxxi] The *flechas* eventually led us to the municipal *albergue*, nestled within the city's walls on the corner of a narrow street we crossed just after crossing the gate. Unlike the rustic, old schoolhouses of Asturias, this albergue was clean and sleek. As we entered, the floor tiles were shiny and smooth, with glass doors leading to a foyer with IKEA style chairs and tables. The *hospitalero* sat at a desk behind a glass window—like the Border Patrol agent did when we entered the country.

We approached the window.

"Credenciales," he said, continuing to read the newspaper as he spoke. *Hospitaleros* in Galicia were—I learned—civil employees, not volunteers like in Asturias.

We paid him the six euro fee—the same fee for all municipal *albergues* in Galicia—and he stamped our credentials and handed us our mattress covers—cheap, nylon sheets wrapped in plastic to cover our mattresses. We grabbed our *mochilas* and headed upstairs to the sleeping room—a large, rectangular room with twenty-two metal-framed bunk beds. It seemed as if all of the beds were occupied. The sun, the weekend, and last one hundred kilometers had brought a new crowd of faces.

Lugo marks one hundred kilometers (62 miles) from Santiago, and this last hundred kilometers attracted new pilgrims, as it is the closest a pilgrim can walk from to get to Santiago and still get a *Compostela*—an official document from the Pilgrim's Office in Santiago verifying one's pilgrimage. I called these pilgrims 'Ultimo Cien-kilometristas,' or 'Last one-hundred kilometeriststs,'—pilgrims who join at the last minute just to get a Compostela.

After locating two of the few remaining beds, Cory and I laid our claim. Shortly thereafter, we found—from amongst the crowd of newcomers—Alfonso, Omar, and Juan—our tried and true pilgrim companions. After showering and changing clothes, Cory and I joined Alfonso, Juan and Omar for dinner at a small tavern outside city walls. This time, I promised Cory I would pay.

We all had dinner in a cozy back room, seated around a family table. After the waiter took our orders, he brought us a bottle of wine, which we passed around. After we finished the first bottle, a second was brought out. Alfonso, in a dry but sarcastic tone, asked me if "*Es pecado*," ("it is a sin") to have another bottle. By then, it was a running joke that any moral question would be brought to me to determine if it were a sin. I returned sarcasm for sarcasm. "*Sí*," I responded sarcastically, "*Es pecado*." We all laughed. Cory, I noticed, had not finished his first glass.

After dinner we all scurried across town to the *albergue*. We had stayed out until nine forty-five, and the *hospitalero*—the Border Patrol agent—assured us that the doors closed at ten o'clock sharp. If they closed before we arrived, we would be left to sleep elsewhere. None of us wanted to test him. As we walked briskly through town, we passed the Cathedral, a towering forty-five feet high edifice. This Medieval work of architecture—adorned with ornate bell-towers and well-preserved statues of Peter and Paul—rivaled Oviedo in artistic detail. "Wow," Cory said, as we passed it, expressing for the first time a reaction to a religious piece of art. Though unable to stop and admire the Cathedral that night, Cory and I agreed to pay a visit the next day.

The next day Cory and I were—as usual—the last to depart from the albergue. Our not-so-friendly *hospitalero* came to shoo us out early in the morning as we packed our *mochilas*. After a brief stop at a nearby café, we went to the Cathedral. Well rested after a night free from the snores of Arturo—who had left the Way to visit the town of his grandfather—I walked there quietly, slowly waking up from a deep slumber.

Inside the Cathedral, the interior was dark, not quite illuminated by the rising sun. As in Oviedo, Cory was quiet and reserved. I let him lead the way. We first walked to a side chapel, the chapel of the *Virgen de Ojos Grandes* (the Large-eyed Virgin). Tradition holds that to this image Saint Pedro de Monsonzo composed the Salve Regina. We stood in the chapel for a minute before he continued on down the main transept. I followed. At the front altar, an elderly man was setting up for Mass. Cory, noticing him, stopped and looked at me.

"Did you want to go to Mass?" he asked.

"Sure," I whispered.

I took a seat at a pew, while Cory walked around the back admiring the side chapels. As I sat waiting for Mass, an elderly Priest approached me. He asked if I wanted to lector—that is, read one of the Bible readings for Mass. I agreed. Mass began shortly after, and the old Priest had a fast tempo, getting through the opening prayers and to the first reading within minutes. When it was my turn to read, I scooted out of the row and walked up to the podium. As I read, I would occasionally look up to he crowd sitting in the pews. The Mass, I noted, was hardly attended. Elderly persons scattered sparsely throughout the pews. In the back, I noted Cory. He was sitting still, backpack strap held with one arm, attentive but not really following along with the rhythm.

After Mass, we reconvened near the entry door, exited and began our walk out of the city and into the green hills of Galicia. As the sunlight began to heat up, we slowed our pace, occasionally stopping to admire old Celtic churches spotting the mountainsides. On several occasions, pilgrims we didn't recognize passed us up, but we kept our slow but steady pace.

We chatted off and on throughout the morning. Sometimes we just walked in silence, enjoying the first full day of clear skies. Other times, we reminisced about the blizzard that we endured or the blisters on my feet. We did not, however, talk about going to Mass earlier in the morning. Church was a topic on which we both had come to different opinions. As children, we never missed church on Sunday, yet in college, he stopped attending any form of organized religion. I, on the other hand, joined the Catholic Church.

We had, while he was in prison, corresponded almost *ad nauseum* about church and the different perspectives we had come to take on religion. He had been quite suspicious of anything that whiffed of spirituality. When he experienced a change of heart in the halfway house in Baton Rouge, he realized that he had been denying himself a personal search for answers to deeper questions.

I remembered a letter he wrote me from prison. In it, he said that he had spent the last decade, "shattering a belief system without adequate removal of the debris or replacement with a new one." We had been brought up in a strict Protestant home, where obedience to the Bible "once sat at the center of [his] life and heart," but when he left for college he came to hold any form of religion as simply a chain to be broken, ascribing to no real belief system other than a touch of self-destructive hedonism. Believing in nothing but the pursuit of momentary pleasures, he said, had allowed a "dislodged fragment of truth [to] contribute to spending ten years in a self-destructive prison of the mind." Nothing he believed could motivate him to overcome addiction.

After only a few hours of hiking, we arrived at San Roman de Retorta—the small village consisted of no more than a few houses along a dirt road. Our feet sore from several longer walks the days before, we stopped for the day, having walked only sixteen kilometers (ten miles). Cory and I were the first ones to arrive at the *albergue*—a log cabin type house with a sun-roof covered addition for showers and a washing sink. We each staked out a bottom bunk on one of the sturdy wooden bunk beds that flanked the cabin's kitchen in the middle.

After settling into our beds, we showered and Cory offered to do laundry. After about an hour, the *hospitalero* came. A tall, broad-shouldered man with a balding head, he looked like one of my previous college Spanish teachers. He stamped our credentials, collected our six euro fee, and waited for a couple of hours for any more arrivals. As he waited, he walked over to the road next to the cabin and played the *requinta*—a wooden Galician-style flute.[xxxii] Once settled in, I laid down in bed, resting my eyes as I listened to Galician folk tunes.

After a short while, the two Germans and Christian (from Austria)—who we had not seen since Borres—came to settle in. When they arrived, I got up from my resting perch to visit with them as they settled in.

By the time they were settled, it was dinnertime, and I proposed that we cook together. They were more than happy to accept. Prior to cooking, one of them walked with me to the nearby store, some two kilometers away. A tall, stalky blond, he looked like a Nordic logger. In reality, he was from Bavaria. He had driven a forklift for his father's company ever since he finished high school, working diligently and saving his money. This was his chance to vacation from work along with his friend. In less than a half an hour we arrived at the nearby small town store, where we bought eggs, potatoes, olive oil and onions. He insisted on paying and we each carried a bag back to the *albergue*.

Back at the *albergue*, I set to work in the kitchen to cook with our fresh groceries. I planned to cook Spanish tortillas, which I learned to cook in Madrid while living there for graduate school. Completely different from Mexican tortillas, Spanish tortillas are a quiche-like mixture of eggs, potatoes and sometimes onions—often eaten as the main course of a meal.[xxxiii]

After chopping onions, skinning and peeling potatoes—with the help of Christian—I placed both in a skillet with a generous amount of olive oil and turned the burner on to low heat. As the potatoes and onions simmered—perhaps the most crucial step in the preparation—Christian began to put some chopped wurst cutlings into the sauté. I tried to stop him, explaining to him that meat would have to be placed after the potatoes were sautéed and eggs were added, but he didn't understand my English. I certainly didn't speak German. I called the Logger, who came and translated. The exchange seemed awkward. I could tell that he was trying to tell Christian diplomatically to keep his hands out of the pot. Christian seemed upset, although he repeated "Kein problem, kein problem" taking his hands of the can of meat.

He was about to walk off when I stopped him, demonstrating with my hands what I was trying to do—first cook, the potatoes and onions; then pour the eggs; then put in the meat. He seemed more understanding as I hand-gestured the process. After a patient potato sauté, adding of eggs and delicate flipping the mixture, we added the wurst cutlings. What resulted was the most delectable, wurst-filled tortilla cake. "Ok, ok," Christian said—in a thick Arnold Schwarzenegger-sounding accent—said, "you are the man." I shook my head and chuckled. We all enjoyed a slice of tortilla and a loaf of bread before heading to bed.

The next day we were greeted with bright sun shining into the windows of the cabin. The doors to the cabin open, I woke up to chirping sparrows outside. The German-speaking trio was out the door just as I rustled out of bed. Left behind were just me and Cory—who was still asleep. With no hurry to depart, we took our time waking up, folding our clean laundry, rolling our sleeping bags and packing our backpacks.

Before departing, I sat down on a bed and pulled out my guidebook from my *mochila.* Looking at possible *albergues* along the Way to stop at, I proposed that we sleep that night in As Seixas, some 10 kilometers (6 miles) from San Roman. While a short walk for the day, this would bring us six kilometers from Melide. We could stop there for the lunch the next day, I proposed, on our way through.

Cory, standing in the doorway with his *mochila*, shrugged.

"That's kind of short to walk in a day," he said, nonchalantly.

"I know," I said, "but it's better than sleeping in Melide."

Melide is the point of convergence of the Primitive Way and the French Way, and with easily ten times the number of pilgrims passing through—many of them last one-hundred-kilometerists—the walk would be more crowded, less personal and more commercialized, I told him.[xxxiv] I suggested we take a short day to As Seixas then walk as much as we could of the remaining fifty kilometers to Santiago the following day.

"Well," he said, "I'd rather just see how things go."

At that, I dropped the subject. I did not think he understood the change in milieu that was about to take place in Melide, but I was afraid of disagreeing with him. I was afraid that another conflict as banal as which city we slept in that night would incite an anger, an anger that I had not witnessed in over a decade. I did not under any circumstances want to experience his anger again. I knew he had changed, but in my emotional memory, I worried that he would turn angry for disagreeing with him. The last conflict of preferences we had that was resolved peacefully was when we were in middle school on vacation arguing about what to watch on television.

We began our walk in silence, not talking about where we would stop that day. I could sense a tension between us, however. This was our first serious disagreement so far, and we both weren't used to it.

Around early afternoon, as we walked down a sloped, zig-zag path running down a mountainside, we came across a blond, Northern European-looking girl sitting at a picnic table on a slope carved into the hill. Next to her was a large German shepherd, a sign offering fresh strawberries and a structure that I can best describe as a renovated shack. Hungry, we laid down our packs and sat with her at the picnic table. We all small-talked while she brewed us tea and Cory and I snacked on fresh, homegrown strawberries.

She was from Lithuania and spoke perfect English. While walking the Primitive Way, she met the owner of the shack, who asked her to watch the dog while she left town for a few days. Recently graduated from high school and with no concrete job obligations, she agreed to house and dog-sit, meanwhile continuing the community service to provide refreshments to pilgrims.

As we chatted, she abruptly stopped what she was saying at some point and looked at me directly:

"Are you okay?" she asked. She could sense that I was upset.

"Why do you ask?" I said.

"You look sad," she noted.

"Actually, I am not well," I said, sarcastically. "I was just thinking of checking myself into the hospital."

"You're funny," she said, smiling.

"Just kidding," I said. "Just being pensive."

At that we decided to pick up our mochilas and keep walking. As we were heading off, she stopped us.

"Wait, I'll walk with you."

She and the dog ran to catch up with us. She hadn't had any visitors for the day. Many passed by, but few knew what to think of her sign. She and the German shepherd walked with us both for a couple of kilometers before hugging us both and bidding safe travels.

Cory and I walked for another one or two kilometers (about a mile) before arriving at As Seixas. This was the stopping point I had proposed. Cory walked ahead, with no apparent intention of stopping. Hoping to stall our advance, I proposed we stop for cold water and espresso.

We had just passed by an old ranch-house converted into restaurant/albergue.

Cory followed me along.

The restaurant nearly empty, we sat at an unoccupied table. The waitress came and took our order and then left.

We then sat in silence.

This was the point where we would have to decide where to sleep that night. I could just go along with where he wanted to go, but I did not want to back down. I did not want to sleep somewhere where we would regret. To argue with him civilly, however, meant that I had to face my fears—even if that meant being vulnerable.

***

Padua, Italy
May 2012

Towards the end of my graduate school, Cory wrote me a letter. This was the first time we had communicated since we last saw each other in Marksville. He had not remained in touch because he "felt ashamed not to have a good report to give."

While under probation, he described a spiral into drugs and alcohol, one that was fueled by his anger. As the Bureau of Prisons exerted more and more control over his life—tracking his movements with an ankle brace, subjecting him to a battery of psychological testing and sending harsh probation officers to reprimand him—his ire against the justice system deepened. His anger would turn inwards, he said, as he would blame himself for all the wrong he did. He would then seek escape through drugs and alcohol, which hurt his chances for recovery, he knew, but which he thought he deserved.

Then he was able to forgive himself.

In doing so, he found reason to recover. He believed himself worthy of a sober life. Prison, moreover, would provide him a sober environment in which to mature. "It was like getting back on the interstate after having taken the wrong exit and getting lost in a subdivision for thirty minutes, only to find the traffic had subsided and the detour wouldn't actually have slowed you down much."

"In a divine twist of fate," as he described it, he found in his "shackled existence…a golden opportunity." Prison, he said, provided him the "certainty of solitude I have been needing to achieve certain goals," namely "to pursue knowledge and suffer the often extensive pain of assimilation into wisdom."

Reading his letter, I felt—at first—ashamed. My own brother was not only in prison but in solitary confinement. For several days, I could not stop thinking of him in a deep, dark Medieval dungeon. I was in Padua at the time, finishing my last semester of graduate school in medical ethics, and I remember going to class at the Palazzo Bo—where Galileo used to give classes—imagining a Medieval version of my brother shackled in an Inquisition Prison. Cory, like Galileo, had come under present day society's harsh disapproval.

Yet, the immediacy of his words could not but lead me to believe that this change of scenery was for him redemptive. He had found a much-needed source of inspiration. While regrettable that he had to spend his time in such a deplorable state, it was for him "the extensive pain" he needed to provide a sober place, free of distractions to read, write and pray—none of which he did consistently in the outside world. While 'free' and sober during probation, he struggled with the chains of addiction. He needed a change of scenery.

***

As Seixas, Galicia
May 2, 2013

Seated at the bar in As Seixas, I took a sip of my espresso. Cory, seated across from me was silent, watching the television above the bar. After a minute or two, I broke the silence.

"I think we should stay here," I blurted out.

Then I explained again why I did not want to stay in Melide—large crowds, harder time finding a bed, and the less personal environment. He looked at me, intently, not saying a word while I spoke.

We then sat silent.

My heart pounded—just like it did when I pushed him in the laundry room. I worried that he would get angry, yell at me, or just run off.

He sat still, however.

After a couple of minutes, he spoke.

"I'm just not ready to stop," he said bluntly. "We haven't walked very far."

He was slow in articulating his words as if he were thinking about every one of them.

"If you want to stop here," he said, "go ahead, but I'm going to sleep in Melide."

I pondered his words for a few minutes, sipping my espresso several times as I tried to think of a compromise. Then I reached to my *mochila*, lying on the ground next to my chair, and grabbed my guidebook. Hoping to find perhaps another place to sleep outside Melide on which we could compromise, I turned to the current day's *etapa*. As I opened up the book, I pulled out the devotional card Father gave me in Oviedo. His words came to mind.

Then I realized that Cory was right.

He wasn't trying to be oppositional. Stopping just didn't make sense. We had only walked 10 kilometers (6 miles), and the day was young, the sun shone brightly and we were full of energy. To stop this early in our day's walk would have interrupted the natural rhythm of our bodies. Even if following that rhythm mean going into a crowded Melide, we had to follow where our *Camino* took us.

It was time for a change in scenery—a new *etapa.* I needed to follow my body's rhythm, even if it led me to a large city. I, like Cory, still had plenty of energy to keep walking. I was thinking too much, trying to hard to make the Way easy. I needed a change in scenery. Every pilgrim, I realized, goes through wilderness to get to the city, just like after rain comes the sun. No *etapa* is the same, and each day's new sights provide new stimuli for different feelings. This was the time to go where the next *concha* or *flecha* led me.

"Alright, we'll go to Melide," I said.

He smiled, not saying anything.

At that I picked up my backpack, went to the register, paid for our drinks and headed out.

He followed.

Eventually, he outpaced me. We would meet at the albergue in Melide. I walked the rest of the Way there alone. The sun was finally shining.

10.
Through The Back Door

'J'ai passé dedans la porte d'en arriére'
'Then I went through the back door'
—D.L. Menard

Melide, Galicia
May 3, 2013

Since our departure from Melide, the crowds picked up. After the convergence of the Primitive and French Ways, pilgrims, none of whom we managed to get to know, were passing us up several times an hour. Towns seemed to blend together. With bars and *albergues* spotting the entire walk, we never knew when one town ended and another began. Souvenir shops and travel agencies cropped up more and more. The walk had become more of a tourist hike than a pilgrimage. Cory agreed that "it feels really different now."

Cory and I both agreed that after Melide, we would stick together. If not, we realized, we would get lost amongst the masses. The night before, after our talk in As Seixas, we both arrived at Melide separately. As a result, he managed to get a bed in the municipal *albergue* while I didn't. I slept at a nearby hotel, I felt out of place as I unpacked my bag alone and returned from the shower to an empty room. When we went to Pulpería Ezequiel[xxxv] that night to eat *pulpo*—chopped octopus tentacles a specialty of Melide—we agreed that we would walk together until Santiago. After Melide, he quit his usual running ahead. We walked within talking distance form then on.

As pilgrim crowds thinned out later in the afternoon, Cory and I continued to walk, slowly and steadily. We made a brief stop for water at a bar in Arzúa—a town of twelve thousand people some twelve kilometers past Melide—but then continued on our way. By that point in the day much of the pilgrim traffic had died down as pilgrims checked into *albergues* to shelter themselves from the sweltering afternoon sun. For two tan Texas boys, however, the walking conditions were perfect: eighty degrees and sunny. We continued on at our turtle's pace until we couldn't walk any more. By the time the sun had set, we were at the albergue of Santa Irene, a two-story converted house along the highway just twenty-two kilometers (thirteen miles) from Santiago. We were, to our surprise, the day's first arrivals.

***

Cajun songwriter DL Menard's song 'La Porte En Arriérre" has been called the Cajun National Anthem.[xxxvi] In the song, Menard narrates in Cajun French a series of drunken revelries, after each of which he comes back home through the back door—too embarrassed to enter through the front. While the adventures seem silly at first, they recount a coming of age by the singer as they tell of lessons he learned from his foolish youth.

What makes the song Cajun, in my opinion, is not the reference to drunken revelries but the reference to the back door. Every Cajun household—at least the ones I went to growing up—has a back door that the family uses to enter the house. Growing up, I can never recall a time when we visited grandparents, aunts, uncles or cousins and didn't use the back door. To go through the back door signified a certain commonality of living spaces. Knocking on the front door was not common for family. It was simply too formal.

Perhaps this is why Cory and I didn't enter the Cathedral of Santiago the way most pilgrims do, through the 'front door,' the *Portico de Gloria* ("The Portico of Glory").[xxxvii] This is the one that Martin Sheen entered on the movie *The Way* (2010), the entrance with the famous sculpture by Matteo Giovani through which pilgrims in the Middle Ages were known to enter on their knees in reverence. We didn't even go the first day to the *Plaza de Obradoiro*, the plaza from which the spires of the Cathedral can be seen. In part, this seemed too auspicious for us. We just happened to wander elsewhere once we got into the city.

After an early morning hike from Santa Irene, we arrived to Santiago by mid-morning. We first went to the Office of Pilgrims. Noting that there was no line to get a Compostela, I suggested that we line up. (The lines were known to wrap around the entire block as pilgrim traffic picked up.) Within fifteen minutes we had our *Compostelas* in hand. While I did not go to the same desk as Cory to get my Compostela, we both came back with the same type of Compostela. That means that he stated that his motivations for walking the pilgrimage were "religious," as a different certificate is given to pilgrims who state their motivations as "not religious."

Compostelas in hand, we entered the Cathedral through the façade of Praterías in the Southern transept. This was—I told Cory—the back door. Taking off my poncho and shaking off the rain—which had again picked up through the morning—I felt as if I had just come in the back door from the porch after playing outside on a rainy day. It was not a feeling of bliss, awe or relief, just a feeling of familiarity. I had been there several times before, to be fair, but part of it was simply a feeling of being at home. Cory, as well, appeared calm and collected.

I followed Cory as he began walking around the Nave. As we walked, I noticed a line of people around the back altar. They were waiting to embrace the thirteenth century polychrome statue of Santiago dressed as a pilgrim—a pilgrim tradition going back centuries. This was a tradition I had seen pilgrims take part in when I was last there with Amanda, but, deterred by long lines, we never endeavored to take part. With a shorter line, however, I decided to line up. I was curious about the view from higher up on the altar.

"I'm going to line up to embrace the Apostle," I whispered to Cory as we walked around the vestibule.

"You can come with me or I'll come find you," I continued.

He continued at my side.

"I'll come."

We lined up on the north end of the choir. As we stood in line, I wondered if we were the only Roussel brothers to pilgrim to the Cathedral together as brothers. We were, after all, from a family who once lived not far from the Way. Our great ancestor, Jean Roussel, who came to Louisiana in 1722, hailed from the Vosges region of France, a part of the Alsatian mountain range through which crosses a crucial segment of the Way of Saint James for pilgrims departing from the Rhineland. He came from a humble family of Catholic peasants, as far as we know, many of whom were known to make the pilgrimage in the Middle Ages. I wondered if there was even one Roussel to walk the Way, one in whose footsteps we were following.

After a few minutes, we reached the narrow stairwell leading to the statue of Saint James the Pilgrim. As I approached the image, a tear swelled in my eye. It was then that I felt a profound sense of awe, utter humility—not by the image it self, but by the realization that I had stood on the tombs of giants. Directly beneath me—in the crypt—stood the bones of not only the Apostle Saint James but also hundreds of others who had come to admire him throughout the ages. He brought a message of peace and love to the Iberian peoples, a message on which Cory and I had come to agree, even if living in peace and love meant very different things to us. Cory and I had both followed the living here, who pointed us to the dead.

***

Metropolitan Correctional Center, San Diego, California

September 2013

While serving out the end of his prison sentence, Cory wrote me a letter from "the hole." A nickname for disciplinary confinement, "the hole" was a frequent residence for Cory while in prison. He spent likely several months of his year in prison there. Typically the residence for criminals too dangerous for the general prison population, Cory was one of those rare prisoners who would chose intentionally to go to "the hole." Once, he told me, he was sent for stealing laundry from the guards' office—a violation he committed knowing where it would send him. (As he told me, he could always request clean laundry.) Another time, he let a friend borrow his calling card to call his mother—a violation of prison rules. Never an inciter of violence, he would be sent "again and again for general mischief," in which he would purposefully take part knowing full well where he would end up.

To most prisoners, this was a punishment. "They are all killing time," and the hole offered the least distraction. To Cory, however, "the hole" was "precious." As he described, "the whole day becomes—to steal a word from the Christians 'consecrated.'" The "profound stillness" it provided him offered "the perfect place to practice mindfulness and refinement." He would divide his day, as he recounted, "between contemplative writing and studying."

In an earlier letter, he asked me to buy him books on Amazon—the only allowed seller that could ship directly to prisoners. He didn't ask for any particular books but rather asked me, as "the only person I'm in contact with who is a serious reader," to use "discernment" in finding him "the books that my endeavor to stay learning will require."

I sent him copies of several books that had been influential to me: *The Everlasting Man* by G.K. Chesterton, *Portal to the Mystery of Hope* by Charles Peguy, and *Love Alone is Credible* by Hans Urs von Balthasar. He also received books on Eastern philosophy (authors like Buddha, Ghandi and I Chung) and early American thinkers (like Jefferson, Franklin, Longfellow, Emerson and Thoreau). He read all of them, sometimes more than once. To him, this was a "mandatory retreat" to study "how to live excellently." He sought "deeper, more fundamental learning books" than the blogs he had been reading as a prisoner in the general population when he had access to the internet. As he began to study more and more historical thinkers, he noted in the letter the uncanny observation that he was "working in reverse—learning from the living and only later asking…to point me to their dead teachers." He asked me to continue to help him in his studies.

Corresponding with him while in "the hole" convinced

me that we should walk the Way of Saint James. He had found inspiration while behind bars but was in desperate need of a stable example of living a peaceful, non-addicted life outside of prison. I by no means thought he should look to me for how to live, but I knew that walking together would provide us with a simple, safe place to contemplate together.

More than that, our walk would end at the grave of a great man in history. We would learn through the living, who would point us to the dead. Convinced that we should walk the Way, I ordered him a guidebook.

***

Santiago de Compostela, Galicia
May 3, 2013

After embracing Saint James the Pilgrim, Cory and I attended noon Mass. Traditionally called the Pilgrim's Mass, this is the Mass where all pilgrims who arrived are offered a special blessing. For many pilgrims, this Mass can be an emotional experience—even for non-religious pilgrims—as it is a conclusion of their journey—one surely filled with arduous experiences.

For me, this Mass itself was not particularly moving. It was a short, sweet, Spanish Mass with a nice prayer said for our safe return. The *Botafumeiro* was not even swung at the end. Literally a "fume thrower," the *Botafumeiro* is a massive incensory object hoisted by several men that oscillates across the entire North/South transept. Originally used to cleanse the temple of the stench from masses of pilgrims who came prior to the advent of modern showers, the swinging ball of smoke is more often than not a spectacle for visitors to clamor over, film and photograph.[xxxviii]

What was special about the Mass was that Cory and I went together. This was the first time that we had sat together side-by-side at Mass since my grandmother's funeral. Not raised Catholic, he was unfamiliar with when to sit, stand and kneel. He did what he could to follow along, however. During the sign of peace, we found Juan sitting behind and greeted him. Afterwards, we joined him for lunch after Mass along with Omar, who was also at Mass seated elsewhere. Alfonso had continued on to Finisterre[xxxix], Omar told me. We went to Casa Manolo—a popular pilgrim restaurant nestled in the Plaza de Cervantes.

While we were waiting, an elderly man joined our group. A white-bearded, bronze-skinned gentleman carrying his *mochila* with one strap, he bore a surly look like a Spanish Ernest Hemmingway. He was quite boisterous. As we were seated, he pointed to a table in the back that could accommodate five. "We'll sit here," he shouted, in a thick Malagan accent, pointing to two tables in the back.

As we waited for our food, Omar asked if I was eager to return home to see my son. I answered that I was—of course. Juan asked if Cory had a girlfriend—he must have forgotten when Cory told him he did in Borres.

"Sí," Cory nodded.

"That you're not in love with," Omar said. Everyone laughed…but the old man.

"But Landon," Omar went on, "he is in love."

The old man scowled. His eyebrows scrunched and he frowned, saying: "Love is impossible!"

Taken aback, I queried him.

"What do you mean by that?"

"When you're young, you look at your partner who has a mole right here—" he pointed above his lip at his white mustache…

"You look at her face and say 'Oh that's no problem, you're beautiful, I love you the way you are…' but when you get old, you yell at her, 'Why don't you get that mole of your face?!'" he gestured, pointing at me.

I stopped him.

"Wait a minute, that may be one person's experience but that does not mean that it is everyone's does it?" I asked.

The point was lost to him. He continued venting. From what I could follow, he married his wife young but did not necessarily want to marry her. As he's grown older, he's become less satisfied. At some point, I lost what he was saying. His thick Malagan tongue was difficult to discern. Trying to stay involved, I stopped him at the end of one of his sentences.

"What does that mean?" I asked

He said the sentence again.

I still didn't understand.

I asked Omar to translate—still into Spanish, but a more understandable tongue.

"He was with his wife when they were teenagers. They were having relations and the woman got pregnant. So he had to marry her—"

"In that time it would have been unthinkable not too—" he added. "There was no other choice."

"And so did he stay with her?" I asked, divulging how little I understood of his tirade.

"Yes, he stayed with her," Omar said, interpreting the situation in a more understandable Spanish.

"*Eso*," (Spanish for "that's it") said the old man, nodding.

At that point, I gave up trying to convince him. He seemed to have already made up his mind on the matter. To him, society's expectations forced him into an unhappy marriage. How could one hope for love, he reasoned, when it is tied to responsibility, which does not seem to fulfill one's personal need for satisfaction? Our self-interest, seemed to high a barrier to cross in the name of love.

Cory, I noticed, was silent during the discussion. He couldn't comprehend the man's thick Spanish. Cory could pick up maybe half of what was said in Spanish if it was clearly and slowly pronounced, but for this guy's thick, Andalucian accent, which eluded even my experienced listening skills in the language, this was too much for him to piece together.

Hoping to change the topic, I asked if anyone at the able wanted to have breakfast at the Hotel of the Catholic Kings the following morning. Originally a public hospital for pilgrims built by Queen Isabel and King Ferdinand, the Hotel of the Catholic Kings[xl] is now a five-star Parador—a brand of luxury hotels in Spain—that sits in the middle of the Plaza de Obradoiro, the glorious spires of the Church visible form the hotel's second floor. The first ten pilgrims to show up at the garage entrance to the hotel at the traditional eating hours—eight in the morning, noon and seven in the evening—are entitled to a meal. This was a small consolation awarded to pilgrims by court order after privatization of a publicly built facility.[xli]

All—minus the old man from Malaga—agreed to meet there.

***

Hotel of the Catholic Kings, Santiago de Compostela, Galicia
May 4, 2013

Cory and I were the first pilgrims to arrive at the garage of the Hotel of the Catholic Kings. The rain was light but persistent as we sat outside. Police cars pulled in and out of the station just across the hotel in the plaza as we waited. Omar, Juan and several other pilgrims from the French Way soon arrived. We sat for what seemed like an eternity until an attendant opened the garage door, verified our *Compostellas* and led us down a corridor next to several kitchens where chefs labor away at roasting chickens, baking bread and sautéing vegetables. He led us to a small room with a single stone window at one end of the wall. The room was dimly lit with several wall-mounted light fixtures in the shape of the Saint James Cross.

We seated ourselves along a small rectangular table adorned with a white table-cloth. A waiter soon brought us a couple of pitchers of coffee and a tray of *churros.* Noting on the walls framed paintings *Camino* artwork reminded me of the importance of the Way in allowing people to travel in the Middle Ages. Public hostels such as these were the only hope for many pilgrims to survive the trek.

Just then, I recalled another work of *Camino* history—*the Codex Calixtinus.* Written by French monk Aymeric Picaud in the twelfth century, the *Codex* is considered by some to be Europe's first travel guide. The last time I was in Spain, the *Codex* was reported stolen from the Cathedral. Since then, I hadn't heard of it.

"Whatever happened to the *Codex*?" I asked Juan, my proven Spanish history buff.

"They found it. Not long ago."

"Who took it?" I asked.

"An old man who worked in the Cathedral."

"He had thrown it in his garage," Omar added.

"Not only that," Juan added, "he had been stealing from the coffers for years. He stole millions."

Aghast, I asked him what could lead someone to be so malcontented as to rob from the Cathedral.

Juan shrugged. "I don't know. Maybe bitterness."

Omar then changed the subject to the bad weather we endured, asking the few pilgrims from the French Way whether they had endured similar weather. They hadn't. Omar then spoke of seeing Cory running up a mountainside in the rain.

I then recounted losing track of Cory on one of those rainy days, pacing back and forth in Tineo for over an hour to find him.

"A good big brother," Omar said. Then, rhetorically, he asked Cory: "does your brother take care of you?"

Cory didn't quite understand the question, so I translated.

Cory answered in Spanish.

"*Siete años es mucho tiempo*," he answered.

("Seven years is a long time.")

"What do you mean?" Omar asked.

Cory repeated himself.

"He's been studying for so long that we haven't seen each other," he said. He was almost tearful.

Omar, not knowing our past, didn't seem to understand the emotion packed behind those words.

"*Es mucho tiempo estudiar medicina*," he commented. ("It's a long time to study medicine.")

Everybody then kept talking about other *Camino* adventures.

Hearing Cory's response, I was shocked. I had not even thought that he missed me while we were living away from each other. When he was in North Carolina, Austin and San Diego, I just thought that he didn't care whether we saw each other or not. Then it was apparent. During our time away from each other, he wanted me in his life, even if he were occasionally enmeshed in drugs and crime. He actually missed me.

After our leisurely breakfast, Cory and I went to the Café Literarios next to the Cathedral. When we sat down and ordered some coffee, I mentioned to him that I still found bothersome the cynicism of the old man at lunch the day before.

"What exactly did he say?" Cory asked.

I recounted to him the old man's story.

"As a consequence of his personal experience," I said, "he believed that true love was impossible."

Cory chuckled.

"Yeah, that's pretty cynical."

Looking outside the café window at the rain falling in the Plaza, I thought about our correspondence on love while he was in prison. As he wrote me in a letter from "the hole," he thought true love for another was a worthy ideal but one which he could never live up to. How, he questioned, could he overcome his inborn selfishness to truly give himself to another? He had read the diary of Saint Therese of Liseux and hagiographies of Saint Francis of Assisi with admiration but believed that he was incapable of living such high standards as theirs. At best, he said, he could admire them from a distance.

After sipping our espressos in silence for a minute, Juan approached from outside and joined us. We changed the topic.

After a few minutes of small-talk with Juan, Cory and I spent the rest of the day at the Cathedral museum. As we walked through the art galleries, I could not stop thinking about Cory's comment earlier at breakfast.

"*Siete años es mucho tiempo.*" ("Seven years is a long time.")

He said the words with no intent of condemnation, simply as an honest answer to Omar's question.

Yet hearing the words, I could not but feel a twinge of remorse. I questioned whether I could have reached out to him more while he was wandering the mountains of Appalachia or living in downtown Austin.

After going to the Cathedral museum, we visited the *Portico de Gloria* before leaving the Cathedral to meet up with Juan for a glass of wine. We exited the Cathedral to the Plaza de Obradoiro where the rain had stopped. I stopped thinking about the words from breakfast as we left to enjoy our last evening in Santiago together.

***

Santiago de Compostela, Galicia
May 5, 2013

The streetlights were bright as we navigated the paved sidewalks of Santiago's outskirts. It was five o'clock in the morning, and Cory and I had to walk approximately a mile to the bus station from the albergue. The bus would take us to the airport, from which we would catch and early flight to Madrid. Our backpacks on our backs, we walked quietly along the suburban sidewalk beneath a sky now clear of clouds. The stars were visible even with the city lights. This field of stars, this *Campus Estellae*, was said to have guided the Way for Saint Pelagius to the tomb of Saint James in the seventh century.[xlii] The monk would later bring the discovery to the attention of the local Bishop, leading a Way for millions of pilgrims to follow throughout the Middle Ages up to the present day. Generations upon generations would follow this path under the stars.

As I watched the stars glimmer, I thought of how long the light had traveled to reach us. Perhaps five, ten or fifteen years had passed since light left any one of those stars and reached my eyes. I thought of how much had happened between Cory and me in that time period. Seven years can be a long time. I kept thinking about Cory's words. Then again, is it? We had walked across the Asturian Mountains and had picked up as if we had never left off.

As we crossed street, the bus station became visible. The bus to the airport just pulled out. We ran to flag the bus driver's attention. He noted us, stopped and opened the bus door. We boarded the bus, whose bright fluorescent lights obscured for the last time the stars of Santiago. Our Way to Santiago was over, but in reality, we had just begun the next day's *etapa*.

Epilogue:
The Journey Home

After returning to Texas from Spain, Cory stayed with Amanda, me and Benny in Houston for several weeks. Sometimes he would sell bottled water at a busy intersection nearby. Other times he just relaxed, took walks around the neighborhood with Benny and ate meals with us. Admittedly, I did get annoyed with him for sleeping late in the living room of our one-bedroom apartment. Why, I wondered, did he seem so blasé about what he would do next?

Then I remembered Father's words. This was our day's *etapa*. He was living each moment as it came, enjoying time with me, Amanda and his nephew Benny before we moved. I simply asked him to be mindful of when we need to get up, reminding him that he is always welcome to stay as long as he liked. He was more than willing to wake up earlier.

After a few days in Houston, I returned to New York for my last two-week course in medical school. Cory stayed and helped our mom care for Benny. When I returned, he stayed to help us pack all of our belongings into a U-Haul storage box and haul it off to the shippers.

My last memory of Cory in person before leaving Texas for Cambridge was of dropping him off at the bus station in downtown Houston. He had bought a ticket on Megabus on my iPhone—his cell phone battery was dead. Without a pen or paper to write down the confirmation number, he ventured to memorize it. I don't know how many digits it was but more than seven. He offered to pay me back in cash, but I didn't let him. How could I? He didn't even have a home to stay at when he got back to Austin. He didn't care that he was living life minute to minute. He was unencumbered and that's what mattered to him.

***

Cambridge, Massachusetts
October 27, 2014

I had just pulled my iPhone out of my locker after a swim at the MAC Harvard gym in Cambridge when I noticed an urgent text from my mom.

"Please call back now," it read. I called immediately.

"Cory's dead," were her first words.

The first thing that came to my mind was: "thank God we went on the Way before he died." I asked for details but she had little. All she knew was what the Harris County Medical Examiner told her. Cause of death was ruled to be secondary to trauma. More information would have to come from the homicide department. It was thought to be due to a murder, though there were no obvious suspects. Amanda, Benny and I immediately flew to Houston to arrange his funeral.

On the flight there, I read the book of Job, whose words resonated with me. Though upstanding man, his family was killed and his fortune wiped away. I asked, like Job: *how could a good God allow such calamity to happen to him?* He was not perfect, but he didn't ask for this.

Still, every time I ventured to question the calamity of his loss, I could not but look back with gratitude for the time we had together on the *Camino*. Without it, we may never have had the chance to come together after so many years of distance, both physical and emotional. I never expected him to die so soon after the *Camino*, but looking back I realized that our pilgrimage really was—as I first believed in the chapel in Oviedo—a miracle.

Thank you for taking part in my journey, for traveling along with me as a fellow pilgrim *On the Primitive Way.*

If you would like to continue on the journey by receiving up to date information about *On the Primitive Way*, including local events, giveaways, webcasts, and blog posts, visit the book's website at OnthePrimitiveWay.com and sign up under the 'Join our mailing list' pop-up box.

-Landon Roussel

About the Author

Landon Roussel is a three-time pilgrim on the Way of St. James. He has written articles on the Way for pilgrim publications such as *La Concha* and *El Peregrino*. He was inspired to write his first book, *On the Primitive Way* after the death of his younger brother, Cory, with whom he walked the Way just before he died. In addition to writing on the Way, Landon also hosts a blog site, *Communitas Blog (CommunitasBlog.com)*, and is a doctor at *Communitas Primary Care*. He lives in St. James Parish, Louisiana with his wife and two children.

Index

Landon Roussel

Acknowledgements

First and foremost, I would like to thank my wife and two children for their patience as I've written, edited and published this book.

I would also like to thank my mother, father, and sister, Bethany, for their support of my writing. Grieving the loss of Cory has been a trying burden on us all, but by their support I have found the strength to tell our story and in the process have found healing.

I want to thank all of the pilgrim companions Cory and I made along our walk to Santiago. Many lent us a helping hand when we were weary travelers on the *Camino*. In particular, I am eternally grateful to Juan Enrique Serrano Moreno and Omar Fernandez Oña for their friendship, support during the time of the book's writing and participation in the book's promotion.

Furthermore, I would like to thank all those hospitaleros, restaurant and bar owners and *Camino* volunteers who work so tirelessly to make the *Camino* possible. Without them, we would have no *Camino*.

Finally, I cannot express enough gratitude for those who helped make this book publication possible—a special thanks to Christina Rodriguez (Curtis) for her earnest work on the cover design, to Cathy Samuelsen and Ann Livi Andrews for their thoughtful input, and to Harte Weiner for editing.

Endnotes

[i] Located in Canton, Texas, this rural rehab was a several hours drive from our house in Beaumont. The facility took in teenagers with drug problems and provided them an intensive rehabilitation, sometimes lasting months. Patients were not allowed to leave until they were committed to be drug free.

[ii] This was the poster, provided by Spain's Office of Tourism.

[iii] For more on how I came to find out about the *Camino* from this professor, see my article in the *Rice Thresher* written in his memory.
http://www.ontheprimitiveway.com/#!Personal-interaction-with-professors-vital-to-learning/colb/561f782e0cf297bd68655125

[iv] This day was ironically the day that Christopher Dorner, a California police officer who shot three people

in a rampage, was on the run and being chased by Southern California police. The News Alerts almost exclusively dealt with the chase.

[v] Really, the variety of albergues runs the gamut. With over two hundred-thousand people walking the Way of Saint James every year, a plethora of different sleeping arrangements are available to accommodate pilgrims. Most are simple houses with a few large rooms with bunk beds, a kitchen and a shower. Some are just a single large room filled with bunk beds. Some are virtually hotels. Some are public—run by the local government or the local community. Some are private—run by the parish or by private organizations. Some are free, while some cost as much as 10-15€. Some serve full meals, while some serve nothing.

[vi] I've chronicled my reflections on this phenomena in a pilgrim magazine in an article entitled "Que pensar de los ultimos 100 kilometros," *Peregrino*, magazine of the Way of St. James. December 2011. Federation of the Way of St. James: Logroño (Spain). Pages 38-39.

[vii] The Christmas Eve bonfires along the Mississippi River in Saint James Parish now attract visitors from around the country. Stretching for up to 30 miles along the river, bonfires are a spectacle local residents and visitors alike. The tradition of bonfire lighting on Christmas Eve dates back to the nineteenth century and was believed to have been brought over by French and German immigrants to Saint James Parish. (Interestingly, the Acadians who settled near Lafayette do not celebrate this tradition.) Earliest historical records of bonfires in Saint James Parish recount the Marist Priests at Jefferson College (now Manresa House of Retreats in Convent)

teaching families to build bonfires. The religious significance of the bonfires probably dates back to the tradition of lighting bonfires on the summertime Feast of Saint John the Baptist, which was celebrated in France, Germany and the British Isles. Taken from the line in the Canticle of Zacharias that the savior will "shine on those who dwell in darkness," Europeans in the Middle Ages would burn bonfires filled with all the trash they were trying to get rid of, signifying the end of the Old Law with the coming of Christ. How this tradition got moved to Christmas Eve in Saint James Parish is still unclear. For more information, see: http://www.louisianafolklife.org/LT/Articles_Essays/SFbonfires.html https://www.catholicculture.org/culture/liturgicalyear/activities/view.cfm?id=303

[viii] Blind River is a waterway originating from Maurepas Swamp Wildlife Area of Saint James Parish, just west of New Orleans. Beginning at approximately five miles inland from I-10, the river is lined with vacation condos built on stilts known as 'camps.' My grandfather, Paw-paw, had a camp there, called 'Lagniappe' (French for 'a little something extra') that we used to visit as children.

[ix] The *retablo* in the Cathedral of Oviedo stands nearly two thirds the height of the roof. Divided into twenty-three scenes, its carvings depict the Infancy, Public Ministry, Passion Death and Resurrection of Christ. Commissioned by Bishop Valeriano Ordóñez de Villaquirán in 1512, it serves as a prime example of the didactic purpose of Medieval art—a means by which to teach a largely illiterate population.

[x] The Capilla de Nuestra Señora del Rey Casto was originally founded by King Alfonso II, "the Chaste," in the ninth century. It is the first pantheon of the Spanish monarchy, and various Asturian kings are buried there. The doorway to the main sanctuary, bearing the figure of the Virgin and Child flanked by the apostles James and Peter (on the right) and Paul and Andrew (on the left), was constructed in 1470 by Juan de Malinas.

[xi] The Virgen of Covadonga is believed to have granted victory to Asturian soldiers in the Battle of Covadonga against Moorish invaders in 722. Victory in battle was attributed to her intercession. After that a shrine was build in her honor and she was named Patroness of Asturias. As a result of their victory, pilgrims were able to travel through the region with a relative degree of security, making it possible for the first pilgrims to walk this route from Oviedo. Hence the name the Primitive Way.

[xii] Seashells and yellow arrows are essential to finding one's way to Santiago. Some seashells are hundreds of years old, while some are more recent. Most of the painted yellow arrows have been posted within the last twenty years. These way-markers can be found anywhere from on the ground to high up on a city-building, from a public park to on someone's house. without hundreds of miles of ubiquitous trail markers, all put up by the goodwill of local communities, pilgrims would easily get lost or spend all days asking around for the right way there.

[xiii] The Order of Malta was originally founded in 1048 as an order devoted to the protection of pilgrims and as

such would build churches that could also serve as places of shelter for pilgrims along the Way.
http://sanxuanvillapanada.blogspot.com/p/historia.html

[xiv] Built in the 1920's by Antonio's grandparents, whose black-and-white portrait sits on the wall to the right of the bar, *La Pacita*, named after his Cuban grandmother Maria Abello de La Paz ('La Pacita') quickly became an icon for the village. Major events in town like weddings, funerals, and liturgical feasts were all held at La Pacita. The family business nearly closed, however, when Antonio's grandfather was rounded up and shot outside the village during the Civil War, leaving his grandmother to take care of his mother—just a baby at the time—while still running the business. Amidst the tragedy of losing her husband, Maria Abello rose to the occasion of keeping in business, soliciting the aid of her sister, who helped her keep the place running until their retirement in 1995. Operations were then left to Maria Abello's niece, until her grandson Antonio returned home from work elsewhere in the country to his home village in 2010 to run La Pacita. Continuity of tradition brought him there, even as the economic crisis that hit the country in 2009 threatened the business.

In fact, in some ways the economic crisis had helped Antonio. For by the time he arrived at Las Dorigas, La Pacita had become home to a new tradition: providing food and lodging to pilgrims on the *Camino* Primitivo, a tradition which had only increased in participation during the crisis.

As the number of pilgrims on the French Way of Saint James steadily began to rise in the beginning in the 1990s, the Primitive Way, in turn, also picked up in popularity for those seeking an alternative to the massive crowds of the French Way. La Pacita, situated prominently along the Primitive Way, naturally benefitted from the increase in the number of pilgrims, even if they were often unemployed young adults who only had single euro coins for coffee.

[xv] Built in 1024 by Princess Christina Bermudez, child of the King of León, a region of Spain, the monastery served as a site of religious life for the princess after the death of her husband. When she died, the monastery was bequeathed to her survivors, who in 1120 donated it to the Order of Cluny, the medieval order largely responsible with the spread of monasticism throughout Western Europe. With Cluny, the monastery grew, until the Cluny monastery lost its influence in the thirteenth century and gradually lost control of its monasteries. After the departure of Cluny, the monastery fell into different hands of feuding nobility until the Benedictine Congregation of Valladolid acquired it in 1536, under whom it would remain possession until state seizure by the Napoleonic government just after the French Revolution.

[xvi] Casa Pachon is one of those restaurants on the Way whose mission is to serve hungry pilgrims. Not every restaurant finds in serving pilgrims a charism, but this is what they do and they do it well.

[xvii] This statue is actually a solar clock. When it is not raining, the pilgrim's shadow points to the hour. Inaugurated in 2004, a Holy Year (a year in which the feast of Saint James, July 25, falls on a Sunday), this "Monument to the Pilgrim" was built in honor of pilgrims who walked the Primitive Way of Saint James.

[xviii] The relationship between Pope John Paul II and General Franco is far too complex for me to comment on with any authority, other than to say that the Pontiff was careful not to support or condone the fascist government.

[xix] I am no expert in Spanich economics, but as I understand the situation, Spain's regional governments spending have a considerable degree of autonomy in their budgets, resulting in a not uncommon scenario where local governments spend far more than they can afford and—to the chagrin of the Federal government—not uncommonly find themselves deep in debt.

[xx] The Nueva Allandesa at its inception was not known for its food. When its founder Encarnación Fernandez bought an old eatery called La Pola in 1957, the place was not known for any particularly special cuisine. Looking to re-vitalize the place and develop a niche for serving local dishes, she dug a recipe for stuffed cabbage from an old Asturian cookbook, as it allowed her to make use of local vegetables from the nearby mountains. Along with her sister Pura, co-owner of the eatery, they learned to perfect the temperature and length of time needed to keep the vegetables tender and flavorful, an art which Encarnada came to appreciate after eating daily overcooked vegetables while hospitalized for several months in Oviedo with asthma. At the start, however, vegetable-infused medleys were too much of an aberrancy for many Asturians to try. That is, until Pura's son Toñin began to charm them with his personal guarantee that 'if you don't like it, we will change it without a problem.' Thanks to Toñin, la Nueva Allandesa gained fame for its *pote asturiano* and stuffed cabbage.

[xxi] A small, gothic structure built in the sixteenth century, the Church of Saint Andrew is home to a sixteenth century, three-level Renaissance retablo at the head of the sanctuary, flanked by two side chapels, the right one of which houses a fourteenth century Romanesque statue of Our Lady of Hazel, patroness of the region. Devotion to Our Lady of Hazel traces back to a legend in the ninth or tenth century in which shepherds found an image of the Virgin Mary in the branches of a hazelnut tree, a tree that had been regarded by the Celts in the area as sacred. When the shepherds found the image, they hung it in the nearby church, only to find it disappear overnight and re-appear the next day amongst the same tree's branches. After several successive nights of removing the image from the branches, hanging it up in the parish church and finding it the following day nestled in the same tree, the local rulers decided to erect a chapel in that very location.

It was to this shrine, thought to be located on a hill just outside of Allande that French pilgrim and author of 'Le Chemin de Saint Jacques Monsieur' Gascon Pierre Villafloure visited in the Middle Ages. Having fallen ill from perpetual bleeding in the mouth, M. Villafloure reports being nearly bedridden for forty days in Allande. During that stay, one of the monks from the monastery in Cornellana urged him to pray at the shrine daily for his healing. Legend says that he was healed, and after his recovery, he prayed daily for the rest of his life to Our Lady of Hazel.

[xxii] Martin Sheen's *The Way*—According to IMDb, the movie is about "A father [who] heads overseas to recover the body of his estranged son who died while traveling

the "*El Camino de Santiago*," and decides to take the pilgrimage himself." I could not stop thinking about the movie as we walked through the snow. The son, played by Emilio Estevez, died under similar circumstances. While en route to Roncessvalles from Saint Jean Pied de Port, the weather in the Pyrinees had taken a dramatic change, and he wandered off the Way and presumably fell off a cliff. Images of Martin Sheen spreading his son's ashes along the Way filled me with fear that my father would in Mr Sheen's role should we pass away. Not about to let that happen, I took a careful look at each step in front of me, to make sure that there was solid ground beneath the snow, and I did not let Cory get more than ten feet ahead.

[xxiii]Perhaps no larger than a hundred square feet, the Chapel of Saint Mary of Buspol, built in the 1300ss, is built of slate masonry on the rooftop and a rectangular marble slab at its foundation. At the far end of the chapel is a belfry, housing a church bell from 1327, one of the region's oldest. On the other end is a tryptic, guarded by a blue gate at the entrance to keep out foot-traffic. Observable from a short distance away through the gate were three polychrome carvings inside wooden urns: Saint Anthony of Padua, Saint Mary Magdalene, and Saint Marina, an eighth-century Syrian monk.

[xxiv] The Salime Resevoir resevoir houses a 123 foot-high gravity dam, which generates hydro-electric power from the melted snow running off the mountains.

[xxv] Hotel las Grandas. While it is not uncommon to find three or four star hotels along the *Camino* on the French Route, it is exceedingly uncommon to find them on the Primitive Route. This one would count as one of only a

handful of 'luxury' places to stay while trekking the mountains of Asturias.

[xxvi] Mount Saint Alphonsus was built on the West Bank of the Hudson River between 1904 and 1907 by Redemptorist fathers. An order founded by 16th Century priest Alphonsus of Ligouri, the Redemptorists devoted themselves to reaching underserved, typically rural populations just as Alphonsus did for poor shepherds north of Rome. The 92 bedroom facility was originally a seminary for Redemptorists, but after declining numers of new seminarians, the community moved its theological training to Washington DC. In 1987 the Redemptorists began a retreat ministry there, which continued until 2012, when due to declining funds, they were forced to sell the property. It has since been acquired by the Bruderhof community for use as an educational center for its children and for use of its farm land.

[xxvii] Gîtes are rural houses in France specifically designated as vacation homes. It is a thriving tradition in France for city-dwellers to escape to a local gîte.

[xxviii] Archbishop Peter Rosazza, to whom I am eternally grateful.

[xxix] Forty feet high and five feet deep, these walls circle the entire old town of Lugo and are passable only by specific gates. Dating back to the third century, these walls served as protection from invaders throughout the Roman era and in the Middle Ages.

[xxx] Certainly some pilgrims were already walking to Santiago from Asturias to venerate the Apostle once his body was found in the eigth century, but Alfonso II is considered the first pilgrim because he inaugurated the walk as an official act of piety sponsored by a monarch.

[xxxi] Another cause for confusion—the conchas reverse direction in Galicia.
[xxxii] Much like a flute, "La Requinta" is a hollow wooden instrument with holes drilled in the side to let out certain notes.
[xxxiii] The most difficult part of making Spanish tortillas, in my opinion, is flipping the casserole. It takes a special art to flip an egg-potato quiche without the bottom breaking into pieces. The point is to make a flat, smooth topped pie, not scramble eggs.
[xxxiv] For more thoughts on the last hundred kilometers of the Way, see my article written in the Spanish magazine, Peregrino. "Que pensar de los ultimos 100 kilometros" in *Peregrino*, magazine of the Way of St. James. December 2011. Federation of the Way of St. James: Logroño (Spain). Pages 38-39.
[xxxv] Pulperia Ezequiel is nationally known for its octopus. Lines can stretch for blocks on end as people wait for a spot at a wooden table. There is not much on the menu other than octopus. In the front of the restaurant Octopuses are boiled in large cauldrons, after which they are brought to the cutting board and their tentacles are chopped. The tentacles are then arranged on wooden plates and seasoned with paprika and olive oil. Tentacles are then served with fresh, home-made wine and bread to sop up the oil.
[xxxvi] Some have said the song "Jole Blon" is the Cajun national anthem, but with over half a million copies sold, "La Porte En Arriere," has been considered a challenger. Of course, Cajuns don't actually have their own country, but anyone who has spent enough time around Lafayette will affirm that Cajuns have a culture of their own,

unique from the rest of the US. See: https://louisianafolklife.nsula.edu/artist-biographies/profiles/149

[xxxvii] Legends upon legends recount different ways that pilgrims should pass through the Portico de Gloria. A pious tradition has been to only enter the Cathedral through this door on one's knees. Another tradition has been to put one's hand on the scupture of Saint James and shake one's head three times for good luck. This tradition goes back to when the artist, Matteo Giovani, was scupting the work, he would sometimes lean on the pillar and shake his head as a sign of inspiration. Pious pilgrims believed that if they too shook their heads like him, they might be filled with the same divine inspiration. Whatever the tradition, the Portico de Gloria has been ascribed with a special importance for pilgrims entering the Cathedral and as such I have taken the liberty to call it the 'Front door.'

[xxxviii] This massive incensary is one of the largest in the world. It weighs 80kg (170lbs), and is 1.6m (5.3feet) tall. Requiring a crew of men to hoist it to the Cathedral ceiling, it swings some 60 to 70 feet high. For a great depiction of the drama effect of the Botafumeiro, see the movie *The Way* (2010) directed by Emilio Estevez.

[xxxix] Also known as 'The End of the World,' this was for many pilgrims in the Middle Ages thought to be the edge of the earth. While the pilgrimage ends for most in the Cathedral of Santiago, some pilgrims (to this day) believe that it ends in Finisterre. There is a tradition that the Way does not end until one throws their walking stick into the Atlantic. This is partly a tradition that hikers just took onto since the ocean would be the natural end of the

journey, though a certain spiritual significance has been ascribed to returning back to the water.

[xl] The Hotel of the Catholic kings was originally built as a hostel for the many pilgrims who would arrive in Santiago during the late Middle Ages. It was eventually converted into an orphanage, then into a literal hospital. Eventually the Spanish government elected to no longer keep it as a hospital and sold it to the Paradores. Now it is a five star hotel.

[xli] To get a free meal at the hotel, a pilgrim simply needs to be one of the first 10 pilgrims who line up next to the garage (just past the main entrance across from the police station) at the normal eating hours (8am, noon and 7pm) and an attendant will verify Compostelas before leading the group to the small eating room for pilgrims. The food is meager but the experience of being nestled in a cozy corner of this historic building is worth at least trying.

[xlii] There was recently an archeological study done of the bones of the people buried on the hill that Saint Pelagius found. While many people were buried there, it was thought that there was indeed an important person buried there, as evidenced by the orientation of the grave. Revered people were buried at the center around which other bodies were buried. Various fragments of the bones of this person, presumed to be Saint James, are located in a silver chest beneath the statue of Saint James the Pilgrim. While one can not reach historical certainty that this was indeed Saint James the Apostle, who was martyred in Jerusalem, historians have theorized that it certainly is reasonable to presume that his body was

transported through ship-trading routes along the Phoenician coast and eventually to the Iberian Peninsula.

48528009R00137

Made in the USA
Lexington, KY
03 January 2016